HOW I RAISED OVER $1,000,000

KICKSTARTER
SUCCESS

A Tactical Guide to Crowdfunding

ANDREW HAGEN

First Printing, 2018

ISBN-13: 978-0-6483013-1-8 (paperback)

Kickstartersuccess.com

DISCLAIMER

The names, places and events have not been changed to reflect the nonfiction nature of this work. The tactics, recommendations, suggestions and actions in this book reflect what has both worked for the campaigns I have been involved with and what I have learned through personally doing them. While they worked for me, they may not work for your campaign, particularly if you only adopt isolated tactics from within the book.

Kickstarter success is not easy, especially in the Hardware category—if you take on board all of the advice and recommendations within, you will have the best chance of carving out your own successful crowdfunding campaign.

FOREWORD

What is Crowdfunding?

CROWDFUNDING is a platform where you can present your idea or concept and ask for people to contribute some money to assist you in delivering them access to or an early version of whatever it is you are creating.

To help the flow in this book, I use a number of words that are specific to the crowdfunding space that you need to understand up front:

Crowd	All of the collective people using or browsing the platform
Backers	People giving money into the project are getting behind or 'backing' the project
Funding	Process of the backers giving you money
Creators	People receiving the money for their project or idea
Pledges	Money that backers give towards the project as they have agreed or 'pledged' to give the money to the creator
Rewards	Items or products that backers receive from the creator for backing the idea
Ask hurdle	Amount you set as your minimum funds you want to raise on Kickstarter

There are many crowdfunding platforms. However, the one called Kickstarter is the most popular platform. Kickstarter is the one I will refer to mostly in this book as it was the platform I chose to use three times with great success.

Kickstarter has been raising money for aspiring entrepreneurs since 2009 with more than $3.3 billion dollars pledged towards over 130,000 projects. Clearly the platform is popular with over 13.5 million backers choosing to fund a project with many of them repeat backers.

In theory, as a creator, you take the funds the crowd has given you, finalize the development of the product, and then deliver one or more of your products back to the crowd as their reward. If many backers each give a little bit of money to one creator, it can create a substantial amount for the creator to use. The risk for the backers is limited to the little amount they pledged, and at the same time, the creator gets a meaningful sum of money to help them complete the project—brilliant in its simplicity, which is why it is a growing platform to help creators bring us some of the coolest products and ideas on the planet! Here are some questions you might have before reading on:

SO WHO IS ANDREW HAGEN, AND WHY SHOULD I BELIEVE WHAT HE HAS TO SAY?

I am the creator (along with my co-creator) of three successful Kickstarter campaigns that together raised over $1 million for our unique and popular cycling accessories:

Fly6: HD video camera and flashing-red rear-facing light for cyclists

KICKSTARTER

Fly6 Cycling Accessory | HD Bike Camera & Tail-Light Combo

World first bike camera & tail-light accessory to record what happens behind you so you can enjoy the ride ahead.

Follow along!

Created by
Andrew Hagen & Kingsley Fiegert

1,780 backers pledged AU$ 266,594 to help bring this project to life.

Fly12: Full HD video camera and super-bright front-facing light (with companion app) for cyclists

KICKSTARTER

Fly12 Cycling Accessory | 1080p Bike Camera & Light Combo

Cycliq, makers of the world's first rear facing bike camera/light combo, now brings you Fly12 for the front of your bike in 1080p!

Follow along!

Created by
Andrew Hagen & Kingsley Fiegert

1,720 backers pledged AU$ 668,721 to help bring this project to life.

Duo Mount: The perfect accessory mount for your bike using Fly12

KICKSTARTER

Duo Mount - highly compatible and durable bike mount

Super strong, durable bicycle mount. Compatible with 90% of bike computers & (incl. Fly12). Declutter your handlebars!

Cycliq Duo Mount

Created by
Andrew Hagen & Kingsley Fiegert

1,220 backers pledged AU$ 78,768 to help bring this project to life.

Cycliq products can be purchased for worldwide delivery from
cycliq.com

In total, the three campaigns raised $1,014,083. Funding for the projects ranged from 272 percent to 393 percent oversubscribed against the funding goals, with over five thousand units delivered to Kickstarter backers. Our first campaign took two days to hit our funding target. Our second and third campaigns took two and a half hours to hit the funding targets. These successful Kickstarter campaigns have led to a thriving business that ultimately listed on the Australian Securities Exchange (ASX) in late 2016.

The lessons we learned on each campaign led to each subsequent campaign being more effective and more successful, and when I say successful, I don't just mean in relation to hitting or exceeding the funding hurdle, I really mean in delivering rewards (products) to the backers that exceeded their expectations so that they became lifelong fans of our brand.

The products we made are in the hardware category (for Fly6 and Fly12) and design category (for Duo Mount). However, many of the lessons and tactics in this book relate directly to almost any category or any type of Kickstarter or crowdfunding campaign (on almost any crowdfunding platform) you might be thinking of doing.

Having a 100 percent success rate, particularly in the hardware category, on Kickstarter where the average success rate is around 19 percent is something I am hugely proud of. However, I know that it was achieved by following the fundamental concepts covered in this book.

I'm confident that you will find great value in learning these concepts and tactics that I know, when applied, will help you have a great deal of success in crowdfunding your own project.

WHY DID YOU WRITE THIS BOOK?

I have many, many people come to me for advice on Kickstarter or crowdfunding campaigns they hope to launch. I have a standard response for most people: "I have a fifteen-minute summary, I have an hour to hour and a half presentation, or I have a deep dive session that can take around three or more hours. Which would you like?" Most people genuinely interested in building their own campaign, opt for the deep dive, so I thought I'd get it on paper (well, in the note-taking app, Evernote). This book will provide you, the reader, with some of the most effective tactics and processes needed to create your own successful crowdfunding campaign.

You will find other books and a wealth of knowledge on this topic if you browse around the internet. I encourage you to do as much research as possible because you can never learn too much about this amazing system to raise money. In addition, new tools are always being released to help creators of crowdfunding campaigns, so never stop researching.

Crowdfunding is an incredible experience, and yet each campaign differs— different products, different creators and different backers—but there are some fundamental components and tactics to achieve a successful Kickstarter or crowdfunding campaign that I address in this book. Now you can learn and apply them to ensure you have the best chance of success.

WHAT WILL I GET OUT OF READING IT?

Not only will you get a broad understanding of what is necessary to build a successful Kickstarter campaign, you will get specific, tactical guidance on what really fuels a successful campaign. I will show you what goes on behind the scenes to build success well before the campaign even launches. You are here to learn how to craft your own successful crowdfunding campaign, and I want to make sure you not only achieve your funding goal but exceed it by a significant margin.

The business we built from our campaigns is now listed on the main board of the Australian Securities Exchange (ASX), and it all started with the idea for a product five years earlier. To put that journey in context, neither my co-creator nor I had any experience in product development, design, manufacturing, electronics, global sales and marketing, fast-moving consumer goods, distribution, or internet businesses. We were totally lacking in any relevant experience to undertake this endeavor, and yet, we went ahead anyway.

The Kickstarter campaigns (and the $1 million-plus raised) were a fundamental part of the journey of building our business from a simple idea in our minds to a company listed on the stock exchange.

How you use this book is up to you, but at least you should now know that you don't need to have any special skills or experience to forge your own path to success using crowdfunding. All you need is tenacity to get things done and a strong focus on and application of the fundamental concepts I will work through with you in this book.

HOW TO USE THIS BOOK

The experience you will have creating your own successful Kickstarter campaign will be something you will be proud of for the rest of your life. Like many rewarding things in life, they are often achieved by overcoming significant challenges. A Kickstarter campaign is no different—it will challenge you, the creator, in many ways.

Don't let that deter you from starting your own, because each campaign creator will tell you what an amazing experience it was for them and how, post-campaign, they are now better equipped to tackle the next phase of their endeavor. For us, the experience of each campaign took us one more substantial step toward building our multimillion-dollar business that we are now very, very proud of.

I have broken down the book into chapters that I believe need to have specific attention. This is with the exception of the last chapter, which I call "Bits and Bobs." I got that name from a Tupperware box my mother called "bits and bobs," which used to have all the little but important household items that you need but don't have a specific place to be stored. That chapter has many smaller topics that you also need to address but perhaps on their own, they will not be as meaty as the main chapters.

To get the most out of this book, I recommend you follow these simple steps:

1. Read the book chronologically and in its entirety.

2. After reading the whole book, download and print the bonus content (with references found throughout the book) at **kickstartersuccess. com**.

3. Sit down with whomever you are going to work with as your core group to run or manage your crowdfunding campaign with the printed bonus content and rework through the book, chapter by chapter.

For example, you will find that you simply cannot finalize how much money you need to raise in your crowdfunding campaign by reading chapter 9, "Ask Hurdle and Rewards," until you have read chapter 13, "Bits and Bobs," because that goes over some of the important costs you need to consider before fully understanding your product costings, which form an essential part of how much money you have to raise.

While it might seem counterintuitive to have a chapter encompassing one of the fundamental concepts of a Kickstarter campaign, which cannot fully give you the complete answer, you will find that many components are interrelated and weave throughout other components of your campaign.

For example, when we had our first meeting to work out what price should be set for each reward tier (explained in chapter 9 – Ask Hurdles and Rewards) in our third Kickstarter campaign, we agreed up front that whatever we came up with at that meeting would simply be the first version. We knew it would change a number of times as we worked through and refined all the other components of the campaign. This helped set the expectations for the team on achieving the best outcome.

You will find some bonus content for each chapter to provide some additional structure that I hope gives you a little boost in starting your own journey down the crowdfunding path.

Thanks for supporting the book. I would love to hear how it has helped you along your journey.

Andrew Hagen

KICKSTARTER
SUCCESS
A Tactical Guide to Crowdfunding

TABLE OF CONTENTS

WHY

I N THIS CHAPTER, you will explore the reason behind why you are considering doing a crowdfunding campaign. At the end of the chapter, you should understand the importance of the answer behind the question 'why are you considering doing a Kickstarter or crowdfunding campaign?' With the answer in hand, you will be well positioned to achieve whatever is your goal via a crowdfunding campaign.

> **❝ People don't buy what you do; they buy why you do it. ❞**
>
> —SIMON SINEK

This truism flows through to many areas of sales and business. However, I feel it talks directly to you, the Kickstarter aspirant who will need to convince a crowd to fund your dreams. The crowd will back you if they buy why you are doing it.

Why is the fundamental question that needs to be asked before you consider a crowdfunding campaign. There are many reasons for you to be considering a crowdfunding campaign:

- You might have a product concept and are looking to create a business out of it.

- You might just be looking for a quick way of raising some money to help take your product to the next level.

- Do you already have a business and want to apply crowdfunding to your next product as a way of avoiding the usual equity dilution that comes with new investment?

- Are you looking at trying to hit some dollar value cash injection for your business' cash-flow needs?

- Perhaps you want to do it as a 'one off' just to see what happens?

No matter what your reasons, you really need to define why you are going down this path so that you can address all the other components in the correct manner.

If you are looking to do this as part of a larger business plan, then you need to think very carefully before launching a campaign. Like many things on the internet, once you have completed the campaign, it can't be undone. What I mean by that is your campaign will live forever on the internet for anyone to research or find in the future.

WHY IS THIS IMPORTANT TO CONSIDER?

If you think your business might ever need further investment at some stage, consider that whomever is looking at investing in you or your business, will do their research and find your campaign online. Was it a success? Was it a failure? Did you do a good job of it, or was it a botched job? These things will reflect on you both personally and professionally for the foreseeable future. A Kickstarter campaign is quite a public thing to do, and how you perform within it will sit in the public domain for a very long time, perhaps forever. So unless you are doing a Kickstarter campaign for some frivolous reason, I would caution you to plan your campaign carefully and thoroughly. Do not skip any of the fundamental concepts I walk through with you in this book.

Unfortunately, not everyone addresses the fundamentals and not everyone takes the time necessary to make sure they have a success. Following the fundamental concepts within this book and then applying the necessary amount of planning and execution to all of the concepts will give you the best chance of success so long as you have begun by asking yourself why you are doing it and then using that answer as your guiding principle moving forward.

There have been products that have been wildly successful where it would appear that they have not addressed the fundamental concepts, but what did their success mean for them? Look at the Kickstarter campaign for The Coolest Cooler and the Indegogo campaign Skully. Both were wildly oversubscribed, and yet their backers have largely been disappointed because of non-delivery of promised products. I'd call that a crowdfunding fail even though they both exceeded their funding goals.

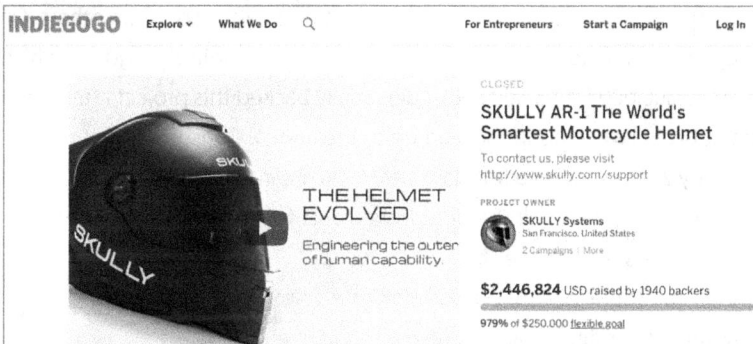

CASE STUDY—WHY

Why did we do our first Kickstarter campaign? As you will read further into this book, I explain more about this. However, the main reason why is best answered by explaining where we were at the time: we had come up with the concept, built prototypes, done two pilot production runs of two hundred units each, and tested our prototypes over thousands of hours of real usage, with great results and glowing reports from users. On one hand, we had real life validation of our concept and product, but these testers were not paying customers, and therefore, we could not base the risk of spending US$300,000–$400,000 manufacturing our first mass production run when we didn't have appropriate validation.

Our "why" was about real, paying customer validation—we wanted to know for sure if customers liked our idea enough to open their wallets and lay down their cash for it. We needed this validation before we were prepared to commit any more serious funds into the business.

It is believed that the founders of the Skully campaign spent funds raised frivolously on things not related to delivering their backers what they'd pledged for. Ultimately, they never delivered any products (rewards) to their backers. Imagine what potential investors would say today to an investment pitch from one of the founders of Skully after the investors do some research and read on the internet that the creators absconded with the funds without fulfilling their promises to their backers?

Even though around 35 percent of campaigns are successful (across all categories), it would be interesting to know the current statistics of how many of those actually delivered the end product to their backers, because I firmly believe that this is the true measure of success in crowdfunding campaigns. Sometimes the reasons for non-delivery are beyond the control of the campaign owners, and even though every effort is made to deliver, sometimes the campaign owners just can't deliver on their promise, leaving the backers disappointed and disillusioned. Failed projects are common, but some get more attention than others. One suck project was a nano-drone called Zano, based in the United Kingdom, which raised over £2,300,000 (US$3,500,000). I personally backed this project after meeting the founders in Las Vegas in the lead up to the annual Consumer Electronics Show in January 2015 (and just a few days before their campaign ended).

This project had all the right ingredients for success: dedicated and passionate founders who were about to get a serious amount of funding that would have, in my opinion, enabled them to deliver on their promise.

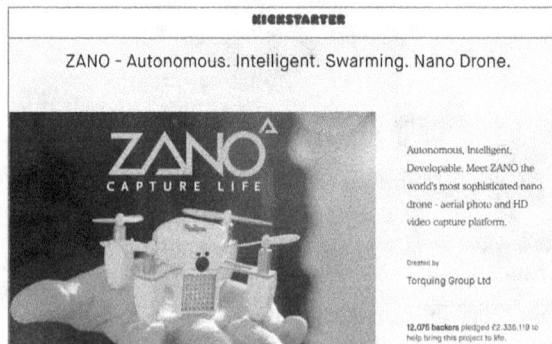

KICKSTARTER

ZANO - Autonomous. Intelligent. Swarming. Nano Drone.

Autonomous, Intelligent, Developable. Meet ZANO the world's most sophisticated nano drone - aerial photo and HD video capture platform.

Created by
Torquing Group Ltd

12,076 backers pledged £2,335,119 to help bring this project to life.

Kickstarter HQ received much negative press about this failed campaign and chose to engage a British journalist, Mark Harris, to investigate this campaign and publish his findings. One of Mr. Harris's key takeaways from his investigation was as follows:

❝❝ *Personally, I do not believe that the creators possessed the technical or commercial competencies necessary to deliver the Zano as specified in the original campaign.* ❞❞

When I look back at our first Kickstarter campaign and consider if we possessed the technical or commercial competencies, I don't think we had them either. This did not stop us from delivering our products to our backers and going on to creating a successful business. I feel Mr. Harris fails to recognize that inventing a new product launched on a crowdfunding platform is most often performed by people who don't possess the technical or commercial competences because they are startups or first-time inventors.

The whole platform of crowdfunding is to enable these types of people to get some funding for projects that would otherwise not be fundable using traditional methods of funding that require evidence of technical and commercial experience. I guess you could say it is why we use this type of platform. The report can be found here: **goo.gl/jGXidv**.

Mark Harris Follow
Mostly British, mostly tech journalist reporting on the US from mostly rainy Seattle
Jan 18, 2016 · 53 min read

How Zano Raised Millions on Kickstarter and Left Most Backers with Nothing

I can only speak for our campaigns and those that I help with in that, as campaign owners, we do so much more than most people know to deliver the best quality products that we can. As an advisor to campaign creators, I only work on campaigns where the creators are genuinely wanting to deliver the end product to their backers. When I consider Zano, I believe the creators were genuinely trying to deliver awesome products to their backers and failed by not addressing all the fundamental concepts I will walk you through in this book.

My hope is that by providing this tactical guide to crowdfunding and highlighting the fundamental concepts that need to be considered, you will have all you need to give you the best chance of success (delivering the products to your backers) for your campaign.

If you don't ask yourself why you are doing it and then you are simply starting a journey with no destination.

Understanding the why will help you arrive somewhere meaningful by properly planning and then executing on that plan. However, if you are trying to create a business and using Kickstarter as the platform to do so, then you still need to ask yourself why you are doing it, write it down, and use this as your guiding principle.

PRO TIP Ask yourself 'why' you are considering a crowdfunding campaign, write it down and let the answer guide you along your journey.

I often ask founders this fundamental question and get answers like, "I don't know," "I want my company to be bought out," or "I want to make a difference in the world." No matter what the answer, without asking the question of yourself (and of your co-founders), it's like starting your car without somewhere to go. I've read many of the sayings espousing the virtues of "the journey" over focusing on "the destination." However, I feel that without a destination to go toward, what direction could you possibly take on the journey?

Of course, during the journey toward your destination, you might deviate, pivot, or turn around, and in so doing, you're still trying to reach out for something. That something is what should drive you and those on the journey with you to do your best to achieve it.

Asking people to help you reach your destination would result in zero help if they couldn't understand where it is you're going. This is no different from seeking investors to asking the Kickstarter community to back your project. Ask yourself (right now), seriously, why are you thinking of traveling this path, and what is the end goal?

With that answer in mind, write it down, commit to it, and take the first step toward that goal. It's going to be a wild ride, so strap yourself in, and let's get going on what can be a very rewarding adventure.

CASE STUDY– WHAT WAS BEHIND OUR LATTER CAMPAIGNS

The why of our second campaign was based on us having an existing startup business that was growing rapidly. While we were making loads of sales, all proceeds were going into growing the business and not enough funds were going into developing new products.

We wanted the Kickstarter funds to help deliver much-needed cash we knew we would have to spend to develop and deliver Fly12 (front-facing camera and light) to our backers. This perhaps is a typical 'why' for a crowdfunding project, but the difference for us was that we already knew how hard and expensive it is bringing a product to production, so we had a very good understanding of what was required for our next innovative product.

We needed the cash to fund development, and applied our Kickstarter experience, pool of engaged fans, and a great product idea to achieve our goals.

The 'why' of our third campaign was twofold. Firstly, it was to offer a product we were already going to produce to our previous Kickstarter backers as a thank-you gift, as we did it at a small fraction above what it costs us to make, and, secondly, to help promote our recently delivered Kickstarter product to a new audience

BONUS CONTENT: Why

After reading the whole book, download the bonus content, print it out, write down the answers to the big question of "why are you doing a crowdfunding campaign?". Have this message at the forefront of the team working on the campaign.

BONUS CONTENT: Kick Off List

This list will give you a high-level view of the key concepts you will need to address as you move through the planning of your campaign. It should provide the framework to plan for any campaign, however, is more focused on a physical or hardware product.

PEOPLE AND WORKLOAD

I N THIS CHAPTER, you will begin to understand how much work is involved in a Kickstarter or crowdfunding campaign. In addition, you will learn how a team of people can help you achieve your goals even if you are a one-person team!

> ❝ *No man is an island.* ❞
> —*DEVOTIONS, JOHN DONNE*

This phrase reflects well in this chapter where you will learn about the workload necessary for a successful campaign and the people you need to help you achieve it.

Your success will be tied to the people around you on this journey, so try not to do it alone. It will be challenging and busy. However, there are ways to make this more manageable, which I will explore in this chapter, providing examples along the way.

Kickstarter or crowdfunding campaigns can add a significant workload to your day, week, month, or year. If you are not prepared for this fact, then whatever else you normally do will suffer.

If you are normally working on your crowdfunding idea full-time or have a full-time job and are working on your idea outside of your regular job, my guess is that you don't have a great deal of extra time on your hands right now. Am I correct? You have friends, family, a partner, pets, or even study commitments that you might be spending some time on. If that is the case and you are thinking of doing a Kickstarter campaign, then prepare for your workload to increase significantly.

CASE STUDY– PREPARING FOR THE CAMPAIGN

I remember writing down all the things to do at the beginning of each campaign and finding it daunting. Many of the things I could see we needed to do would require the help of others which often meant finding funds to pay for them. For our first campaign, there were only the two of us (co-founder and myself) and an outsourced marketing assistant (based in the Philippines) and we really didn't have any spare 'funds' at the time.

With the list of tasks in front of us, all we could do was roll up our sleeves and do it all ourselves. With our second and third campaigns, we had the funds to get things done but we also asked contractors to help out by deferring their fees until after the campaign funds were received. In hindsight, I should have done this more with our first campaign so that we could have achieved more with less.

When I work with founders and inventors wanting to embark on this journey, I always tell them to say goodbye to their partners, kids, friends, and pets! At worst, for the duration of the planning period right up to when they deliver their products to their backers, or at best, a month either side of their crowdfunding campaign.

Yes, it's going to be tough and, yes, be prepared to work hard, but in this chapter, I will offer some advice on how to make this more manageable, so don't be discouraged.

Why, you might ask, is this task going to be any busier or difficult that what you are doing now? Well, for most people, you already are doing something that is taking up your days and what a crowdfunding campaign will do is add to it. Your current day of busy work and life still needs attention, but so will the campaign - it's going to be a challenge, but here is how I suggest you manage it.

No matter how much preparation I have put into a campaign, I always find the extra workload intense. However, the more preparation I put in, the more manageable that extra workload becomes. With three personal campaigns under my belt, the lesson I learned was to bring people in to help and not be afraid of delegating what I might otherwise want to do myself. This lesson, I applied effectively in my last two campaigns, and I found it worked very well.

PEOPLE

One simple and effective tactic is to find yourself a mentor or advisor to review milestones during your campaign. This can be invaluable! Kickstarter campaigns can be intense journeys, and it can be hard to see some of the simple mistakes because you are in the thick of it. These things can often be spotted easily from someone not involved in the day-to-day grind of the campaign.

Find yourself an advisor or mentor, brief him or her on the journey you are about to embark on, and explain in detail why you are going down this path. This will help that person guide you along the way. Ask the advisor or mentor to lend an ear to or review components of the campaign with a critical and independent eye. You will be surprised how easily he or she can spot simple errors when you cannot see them at all. Arrange to meet with your advisor or mentor on a regular basis both leading up to and during the campaign.

WORKLOAD

In this book, I outline the core components needed for a successful campaign. I suggest breaking each one down into timing (when each component needs to be addressed) but most importantly identifying and agreeing who is responsible for managing each core component.

Note also that each component should have a second delegate, as often the components are not simply nine-to-five weekday tasks but often 24-7 necessities. In this case, your second delegate should be able to provide support on weekends or at night.

Obviously, the more people on your team the more manageable this is to do. However, if you only have one or two people in the team, look to get some friends or family to help you out during the extreme needs (day before and day of launch, nights and weekends). Often the tasks are simply responding to backer questions or ticking off the to-do tasks that could

CASE STUDY—FLY6

With our first campaign, I remember having a meeting with the team where we selected which parts of building the campaign each of us were going to manage and then just digging a trench to battle it out. It was grueling work that just did not seem to let up.

not be completed during the week. You, the campaign owner, will appreciate some short moments of respite during the campaign.

When you study other crowdfunding campaigns, you will see that there is generally a period of flatness in the backing activity during the middle of the live campaign.

This was exactly the case for each of our campaigns as you can see the activity charts from Kicktraq for each of our campaigns:

Fly6

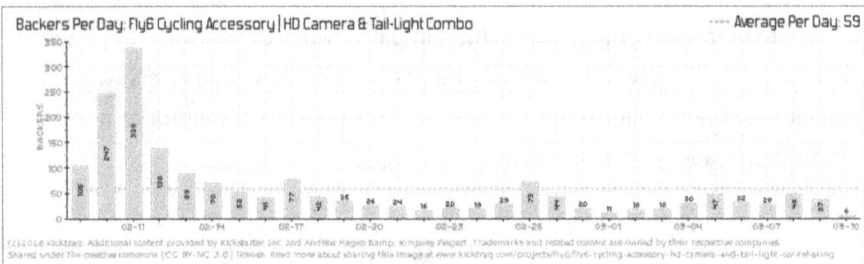

Fly12

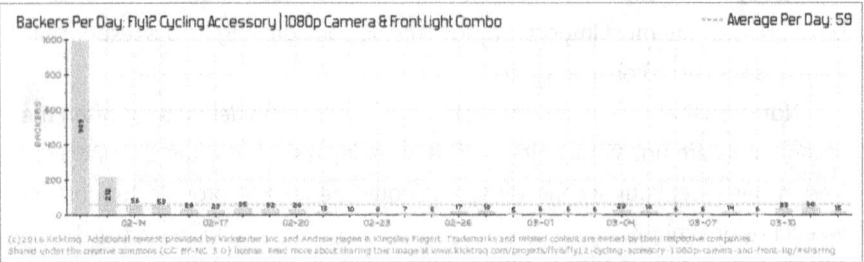

Duo Mount

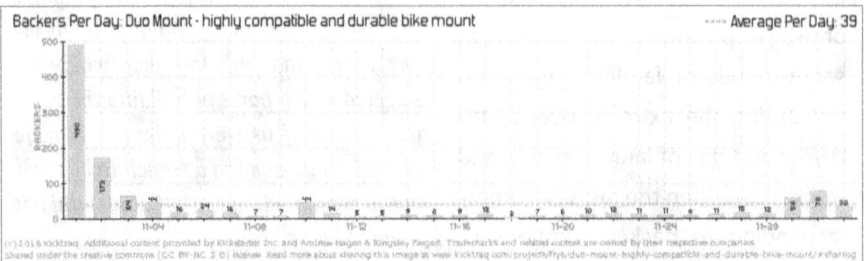

CASE STUDY—DUO MOUNT CAMPAIGN

I remember a few days before we were going to launch our duo-mount campaign (our third one), we found a live Kickstarter campaign with a very similar product, which created competition we didn't think we would have—without continual research and learning, we would not have found the competitor and addressed it within our campaign.

We basically amended our messaging to include how our mount outperformed the features of our competitor. We did this in such a way as to not name the competitor or negatively impact on their campaign.

After the large interest in the campaign up front, there is this very low level of activity in the middle of the campaign. This is always a cause for concern for the creators and usually a time when you hold emergency talks with your cofounders or team to figure out how to get the needle moving again.

We found that, during these times, we came up with some of our best creative ideas to try and revitalize the backing activity. We often wondered why we didn't think of these concepts before the campaign, but perhaps desperate times cause you to draw deep down to achieve your goals.

Responding to comments during the campaign is a very important role and a good example of how people and workload are important considerations when planning your campaign.

It is essential to allocate the task of responding to the comments you receive during the campaign to one dedicated team member. This person must hold the tone and style in a consistent manner within each response to any comments or public questions you receive during the campaign. The backers have pledged for the product you are offering and want to see the same style flowing through the whole campaign. This consistency will help backers have confidence you are going to do what you say you are throughout the campaign, which also builds brand integrity, an important element if you wish to build a long-lasting business.

There was a campaign I researched where the style of language was fairly consistent until some of the commenters started to ask deep and confronting questions. Instead of the same person from the campaign team responding in the same consistent style, the CEO jumped in and posted comments in a defensive and accusatory tone, appearing to vilify the persons making the confrontational questions. This was not a good look and did not do anything to appease the commenters who were asking the hard questions (which they are entitled to do). There is no need to do this if you plan ahead and delegate a person responsible who will hold the tone consistently.

PRO TIP Set the tone, get one person to manage that task or vet all draft responses, and be consistent. It will ensure the comment management will run as smoothly as possible.

After reading through the book, come back to this chapter and have a good think about who is going to be doing what. Get everyone together and work through the main components and subtasks and make sure everyone knows who is responsible for each task and who is the second delegate. Have some backup plans in case someone is not able to do his or her part for whatever reason. The work will still need to be done, even if the delegated person cannot do it.

With our last campaign, we managed this process very well, and everyone knew what needed to be done and who was doing it. With each task, I was the backup in case there was no one to do the task.

BONUS CONTENT: People

This sheet will get you thinking on 'who' is doing 'what' during your campaign. This is critical to ensuring your success. There are many tasks to do, and someone needs to be responsible for each task.

PLANNING, PREPARATION AND RESEARCH

TO BE FAIR to all the other chapters, pretty much everything in this book is about planning and preparation. However, I wanted to go over some specifics that might not land in one chapter or another. I also feel that research and learning should be ongoing—even during your campaign.

At the end of this chapter, you will understand the need for constant research and how that discipline can not only ensure you don't make any fatal mistakes in your campaign, but also help you find that nugget of gold that takes your campaign from good to great!

❝ *The harder I practice the luckier I get.* **❞**

This well-used quote addresses this chapter directly. Each of our campaigns were very successful. However, none of them would have been so if we didn't put the effort in beforehand.

PLANNING AND PREPARATION

There can never be enough preparation, and you can never complete all the tasks that need your attention for your campaign. Let that sink in a little, and then consider that there are so many components to a campaign that not all of them have to be fully resolved or considered.

I often tell people there are about ten to twelve main components (depending on what you are creating) of a Kickstarter campaign and that if you work on and really nail down eight of them, you should have a good chance of success. If you nail all twelve, then you are putting yourself in the best position to have the best success possible. With that said, if you mess up one of the fundamental components, you can equally destroy your ability to achieve any success. Fear not, though, each component is covered in this book, and I will walk you through how to address each one.

PRO TIP There can never be enough preparation, so start now, whatever stage you are at, on achieving your crowdfunding goals.

These 'main components' vary a little from product to product but generally are:

- The human resources you need
- Planning, preparation and research
- Shipping and logistics
- Manufacturing
- Prototypes and samples
- Preparing the media/bloggers/and so on to do stories on your campaign
- How much you are seeking to raise and how much each item sells for
- Marketing
- Your video
- Your campaign page
- Building your list of people who might support your campaign
- All the small but important things I call: "Bits and Bobs"

Some of these things are mutually exclusive, and some are dependent, but all are important ingredients to your campaign, and if you address each one of them (as they relate to your product or project) carefully and spend the time needed to address them, you will give yourself the best chance of success.

If your product is hardware or physical, this will add significant time to your preparation as you look to refine the timing of the manufacturing process so that you

- know when you are going to seed prototypes to bloggers;

- have product samples for doing your video;

- have a working model to meet the minimum criteria set by Kickstarter (having a working prototype); and

- know when you think you will be able to deliver the rewards to your backers.

CASE STUDY– FLY6 CAMPAIGN

With our first campaign, we had already delivered two pilot production runs of 200 units each before we went on Kickstarter. We had a solid understanding of when we could deliver rewards to backers so when we promised June delivery, we were able to confidently articulate that to our backers which gave them the confidence to back our project.

To this day, I think it was the single most important thing we did in our campaign which led to our success—we had prior samples and could prove we could deliver rewards to our backers.

When you work through all of the manufacturing processes (in chapter 5), it should effectively give you the campaign launch date. This will then allow you to work back from that date to understand what needs to be done and by when.

PRO TIP Understand when you are going to have a working prototype and work your preparation schedule back from that point.

Let me give you an example. If you only have a working prototype that does not look like how you envision the final version, you will want to refine how it looks so that when you shoot your campaign video, it looks as good as possible or as close to the final version as you can achieve. To understand when you will have a product that looks like the final version (or at least the final version before

you launch your Kickstarter campaign), you will need to be in close communi-cation with your manufacturer as they are the key to understanding the timing.

Ask them again and again, when they think they can produce this final ver-sion for you. It will no doubt be contingent on many factors that will mostly rely on you, but assuming you can deliver all those contingent factors, this should then inform you of when to plan to shoot your video or when you need to seed the prototypes with the bloggers/media you have lined up.

Wrap this information up, and then you can start to plan many other aspects of your campaign. But, you ask, how do you 'wrap this up'? Spend some time in chapter 5, "Manufacturing"!

WHERE TO START WITH YOUR RESEARCH

The day you consider doing a crowdfunding campaign, immerse yourself in the platform you have chosen. Research all the campaigns both past and present that you can draw information from. They can be similar or very different to what you are proposing; it does not matter. What you are looking for are the ingredi-ents to a successful campaign. Another good thing to do is to understand what does not work by looking at failed campaigns—there is no need to make the same mistakes that others have made already!

If your project is similar to others before you, this can be the best source of what to do and what not to do. You should, through your research, have a good understanding of what your potential audience will like (by way of successful campaigns) or don't like (by looking at unsuccessful campaigns). When you find a relevant campaign or a campaign with a relevant thing imbedded in it, share it with your team and tell them why you think it is relevant as a good or bad exam-ple (e.g., "Guys, check this out. Let's never do that!").

When researching other projects, you are looking to understand the following:

- Simplicity

- Easy-to-understand rewards

- Look and feel, or meeting the cultural needs of your intended audience

- A video that just works

- Is it too polished?

- What is the lighting like?

- Length needs to be just right
- Has it got typical free 'KS soundtrack' or is it original and engaging?
- Is the page too long or too short?
- Is there too much text or too many graphics or too many GIFs?

Try to find five to ten campaigns that seem to work or were successful. Try and make sure most of them are relevant (in some way) to what you are proposing (if your project is a card game, make sure that most of the research is on card games, but don't be scared to throw in a few outliers that have some component you would like to emulate). Make sure the team studies them all against criteria individually and then discuss how your campaign should work based on the collective research.

Use these as the main criteria as a guide for your research:

Video style
Look for lighting, production quality, tone (funny, serious, etc.), length, call to action (was it implicit or subtle?).

Campaign
How much text? How many graphics or photos? Was it themed (focused on the design or manufacturing or the benefits of the product itself)?

Rewards
How many? Did it include T-shirts? Were they simple? Did they have free shipping? Did they include other items (not part of the subject of the campaign)?

Price points
Are you following on from existing products? Try to understand what existing product you are improving on or disrupting and all their price points as well as key features. You need to have a reason why your product is better than theirs for each feature/benefit in your product.

With this research under your belt, you should have a solid idea of what works and what does not work on your crowdfunding platform. With this solid foundation, you should be able to build your campaign so it does not have any cringe-worthy components.

Don't stop researching other crowdfunding campaigns–even after your campaign has launched. You need to be aware of any potential competitors so you can address **PRO TIP** any concerns.

BONUS CONTENT: Research

The bonus content for this chapter is a handy template for reviewing campaigns against set criteria so the whole team is on the same page as they pull together their parts of the campaign you have allocated them.

SHIPPING AND LOGISTICS

THIS CHAPTER is going to give you a high-level understanding of why shipping and logistics are so important to your campaign, as well as leave you with some tactical methods to deep dive into budgeting, which will feed back into knowing how much funding you are looking for. The first question I ask people who want to talk to me about their potential Kickstarter campaign is, "How much does your product weigh?" It seems like such a silly question when most people might normally ask, What is your product? But once you have read and understood this chapter, it will make sense why that is my first question to creators!

I should also preface with an obvious point—it is generally a physical product that requires shipping and logistics (as it relates to getting a physical product from one place to another). If your Kickstarter product is software and a simple link the backer needs to download the software from, then this chapter is not necessarily for you. However, if your software campaign chooses to include a T-shirt or some other physical reward for your backers, then welcome to this important topic. Skip it at your peril.

Why is this chapter near the front of the book you might ask?

Well, it's one of the most important issues that you need to give careful consideration to before embarking on your Kickstarter journey, which can only be fully understood after reading the chapter.

How can it be more important than the inventive or innovative product you are bringing to life?

Without the product you are making, of course, there is nothing to talk about. However, without understanding the shipping and logistics topic, you will be opening yourself up to a potential catastrophic Kickstarter or business failure.

Before we get to in depth, there are a few key terms and phrases you need to know:

3PL—Third-Party Logistic Provider. This is a company that receives your goods (often in bulk) from your manufacturer and then sends them to your customers.

SKU—Stock Keeping Unit. This is a single product type that could differ from another product type by any sort of difference like color, approval jurisdiction, or warranty conditions as examples.

UPC—Unique Product Code. This is a code you give your products (separate to an SKU) that enables retailers to enter your products into their internal systems so they can manage stock, address returns, and apply pricing. You have to use a service provider like **https://www.gs1.org/** to give you UPCs (you often buy a range of numbers for your business) that will work within the worldwide retailing system.

VAT—Value-Added Tax. This is where some countries apply a tax to products entering their country. This is a form of economic protectionism to encourage local (to that country) manufacturing and the economic benefits that come with it. Not all VATs are the same, though! Some countries don't have VAT, and some do. Some have varying VAT thresholds, and some

CASE STUDY—FLY6 CAMPAIGN

With Fly6, we applied a new SKU number with every different model we made.

An example could be where we have exactly the same product with the exception of the size of the microSD card included. In this case, if you had two different card sizes, you would have two SKU numbers.

Fly6 SKU was F6B8GB, which effectively stood for:

- Fly6
- Black in color
- 8Gb microSD card

If we included a 16Gb microSD card, we might have made up a new SKU number of F6B16GB.

You can make up your own SKU numbers, which can be fun!

have varying rates depending on the nature of the item being imported. You need to know all this before you start planning your Kickstarter campaign. Check out the Resources (**kickstartersuccess.com**) for links on how you can learn this topic in more depth.

MOQ—Minimum Order Quantity. This is a number set by your manufacturer as to how many minimum units of a particular product you are allowed to order from them. This varies widely depending on the nature of your product, the manufacturer, their financial capacity, the supply chain, and component availability within the supply chain.

CASE STUDY—FLY6

Our first MOQ set by the factory was three thousand units (less the two pilot production runs). This meant we had to make at least three thousand units at the volume pricing they provided.

Assuming your product is being marketed to the whole world or even a select range of countries and you propose to ship it to these countries, you need to have a system to get your product from where it is being made into the hands of your backers.

Besides the international product approval certificates you will most likely need (which is covered separately in chapter 13, "Bits and Bobs") and the consideration of VAT in various countries (more on that in this chapter), the things you need to consider are the following:

If you are manufacturing the products yourself and you are doing the logistics yourself, you need to consider

- packing;

- labelling;

- shipping;

- package tracking;

- monitoring the process;

- refunds; and

- responding to backers if any problems arise (and they usually do).

If you are making the products yourself and you are looking to out-source the logistics, you need to consider:

- getting the products to your logistics provider from the manufacturer;

- providing your logistic provider with the shipping details (usually in CSV or spreadsheet format);

- paying for the logistic services and when these payments are due;

- receiving tracking details and sharing them with your backers; and

- monitoring and responding to backers if any problems arise (and they usually do).

If you are using a manufacturer and are using a 3PL to manage your shipping, consider these items:

- if you have multiple products/stock keeping units (SKUs);

  - ensuring the boxes have the correct labels for each SKU

- the 3PL knows that you have multiple SKUs (you should have already allocated UPCs for each SKU);

- if your 3PL is in a different country or zone to your manufacturer (like China is to Hong Kong) you need to have your export permits and approvals (which your manufacturer should be helping you obtain or do it for you); and

- the cost (and time) to move the items from your manufacturers factory to your 3PL (in theory at this point you would have already engaged your 3PL and have their service level and shipping rates agreed).

The cost of logistics and shipping will depend largely on three things:

1. Size and weight of your product
2. Value of your product; and
3. Where you are shipping it to

Once you figure these out, the end result will be an average cost to ship your product (given the various countries that your backers live in) and the average VAT allowance

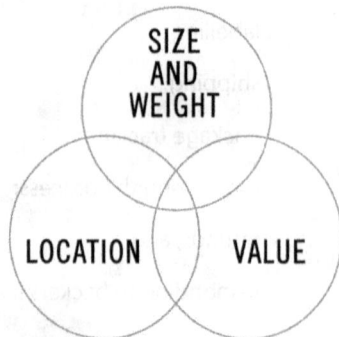

you need to make on each product. This will then give you the shipping and logistics budget item you need for your overall Kickstarter budget.

SIZE AND WEIGHT

Let's start with the size and weight of your product and why this is so important. Shipping rates are usually based on size and weight, so the bigger or heavier, the more it is going to cost you.

For the sake of this example, let's assume you have already worked out all of your pricing and reward tiers to a point where you know your average selling price for your product (this will be covered in more detail in chapter 9, "Ask Hurdle & Rewards"), your number of units you hope or think you will sell and where your target audience is located.

Let's assume you think you are going to sell two thousand units of your product on Kickstarter to various countries or regions and you apply your best guess as to what the allocation of sales are going to be across the countries or regions:

Individual Unit Shipping Costs			
Total Units Sold			2000
Location	% of Sales	Average Shipping cost	Total Shipping costs
US	30%	$20	$12,000
UK	20%	$21	$8,400
Australia/NZ	15%	$25	$7,500
Canada	5%	$20	$2,000
South America	5%	$35	$3,500
Europe	3%	$21	$1,260
Other	5%	$45	$4,500
	Total Shipping costs		$39,160
	Average Shipping cost per unit		$20

Once you have averaged them out, you now you know what to charge for shipping!

This is very helpful if you want to apply a blanket shipping rate to every backer, which can be handy by keeping things simple, but also can be dangerous if you get your calculations wrong.

Imagine, based on the example above, if at the end of your campaign, 60 percent of your backers came from South America (instead of 5 percent). This would mean that you had budgeted for $20 average shipping, but now a major-ity of your shipping would cost around $35. That would mean that you did not allow enough money to pay for shipping, and the difference would have to come out of whatever profit you would make from your campaign.

Figure out what works for you, but the main message here is to know your shipping costs. You will know what to do once you have worked through the detail of the costs, but don't forget to allow a little more than you think as there are many small hidden costs that you only learn of as you are going through the process of shipping. I'd recommend including a 5 percent contingency on what you figure your shipping costs are going to be. Using the example in the table above, I would settle on a budget of $21 average shipping cost per unit. To keep the examples as simple as possible, I have not included this contingency.

How to figure out your overall costs:

If we breakdown the costs of doing the whole campaign at the very highest level, we could get something like this:

- Cost to manufacturer the product(s) on a per unit basis (this could include staff and travel costs)

- Average cost of VAT

- Cost to create the campaign

- Cost to market the campaign

- Average cost to ship units to backers

- Contingency allowance

Using some simple figures, you could work out some costings like this:

High Level Costs	Costs per Unit
Cost to Maufacuter (3,000 units)	$150
Average VAT Impost*	$14
Cost to create campaign (per unit)	$15
Cost to market campaign	$20
Average cost to ship units to backers	$20
Contingency	$20
Total average cost per unit	$239

*See VAT calculation below

PRO TIP Figuring out your costs is critical before you dive too deep into planning your campaign. Without this data, you could fail before you start.

VALUE OF YOUR PRODUCT

If you are going to sell this product post-campaign for $399, you need to offer it to Kickstarter backers for a substantial discount. You need to provide an average sale price to the backers that encourages them to back your project and pledge for one of your products.

This usually is expressed in a discount to the proposed retail price you think you will sell it for. This discount is something you will have to work out for yourself and will depend on many, many factors (like competitors or similar product pricing, value offering, what you think will encourage them

CASE STUDY - FLY12 CAMPAIGN

With Fly12, we averaged around $300 per unit sale price against a retail price point we had selected at $499, which gave an average discount of 40 percent, which we thought was substantial enough to encourage backers to get on board.

The critical thing you have to consider is what price do you need to apply to encourage a backer to pledge to your campaign when they are taking on all the risk of your project with no security—put yourself in his or her shoes!

We found the sweet spot to be between 30 and 40 percent off the final retail price.

to back your project, to name but a few). However, you will have to largely draw upon the reason why (see chapter 1, "Why") you are doing the campaign to give you guidance on your approach to the discount.

For example, if you are trying to raise some money in addition to the costs you will incur, then you need to have the average price closer to the retail price. If you want to sell as many units as possible to build branding or awareness, then move your average pricing closer to your total average cost per unit.

Where are you shipping your product?

If you are shipping internationally, you need to consider the cost of Value-Added Taxes (VAT) that some countries impose on goods entering their country. For

example, in the United Kingdom, VAT is 20 percent for items over £15 in value. This cost needs to be paid, but the question is, by whom?

If you want the product you have sent your backers to land on their door-steps (as in passing through customs) in a country like the United Kingdom, you need to prepay the applicable VAT. If you are happy to pass this VAT onto your backer (and I don't recommend you do this), you send your goods using the delivery duty unpaid (DDU) system that all 3PLs can provide you. If you select this method, after the product is shipped to them, it will be held in customs (in their country where VAT is applicable) until the duty has been paid by the backer.

Your backer will most likely receive a notice that a product for them is held ready for him or her to collect once the backer pays the relevant VAT.

Your backers in these countries expect that the money they have already given you will ultimately lead to the product you offered them getting delivered to their door without further expense.

There are a number of campaign examples, including our first campaign, where VAT was not prepaid and the backers in the UK were not happy with the Kickstarter creators and promptly told everyone in the comments. This is not ideal and can put off other potential backers from pledging on your campaign.

If you select delivery duty paid (DDP), this means that you are taking on the cost of the duty so that your customer has their product delivered to their door and does not get held up in customs—this makes for a happy customer.

There are challenges with each method. DDU could mean a bunch of unhappy customers who give your campaign or business poor ratings that could seriously affect your future business credibility.

Selecting DDP means you need to consider that cost when doing your margin calculations. Using the costings example above, you could potentially wipe out all of your margin if you were to sell into any of the high-VAT countries mentioned without factoring it in.

CASE STUDY—FLY6 CAMPAIGN

Our first campaign with Fly6 we shipped the products out to our United Kingdom backers DDU (without including duties paid up front). This meant that each item got held up in local customs offices until the backer paid the 20 percent of VAT. As you can imagine, this resulted in many unhappy customers who thought they had already paid to have a product delivered to their door. Our main mistake in this instance was that we did not advise them that their purchase price included shipping but not VAT.

They vocalized their unhappiness on the comments section and other online forums, which we addressed as best we could. However, it was not pretty. We learnt our lesson here, and we didn't do that again! All future shipments were delivery with duties paid (DDP).

If this sounds too hard to manage or wrap your head around, then I'd suggest you contact third-party services (I recommend in the Resources section you can view at **kickstartersuccess.com**) who manage international shipping and logistics for many, many crowdfunding campaigns. These services do cost money. However, they take away a lot of pain too!

PRO TIP Deep dive into shipping and VAT consequences as early as possible. The more you understand, the easier it will be to manage.

You could easily increase the shipping amount you charge your backers, but if the amount is too high, this could dissuade your backers from backing your campaign as they are really trying to buy your product for some simple reasons:

1. They want your product before it gets officially released;

2. They want your product for much less than it should cost them when it is released officially; or

3. They are friends or family that want to support you and don't really want your product!

If you add on increased shipping costs to help cover VAT, it is going to turn off the people in point 2, which I feel are the majority of backers. You don't want to place any barriers in front of your main backers. Instead, make it as easy or simple as possible for them to back your campaign. I recommend you cover any VAT by selecting DDP so your backers don't need to worry about how VAT impacts on the delivery of their reward.

PRO TIP VAT is calculated on the cost the person paid for the product (which you need to declare before you send the product to the backer) and the shipping cost combined!

So how do you go about doing this?

Let's look at the effect of VAT on your numbers:

Assume that your average selling price is $250 and that the backers are from various parts of the world of which some have a VAT impost on the product you are shipping.

VAT Calcs				
Total Units Sold				2000
Average Selling Price				$250
Location	% of Sales	Average VAT Rates	# of Units	VAT owed
UK	20%	20%	400	$20,000
Europe	3%	22%	60	$3,300
Canada	5%	10%	100	$2,500
Other	3%	10%	60	$1,500
		Total VAT		$27,300
		Average VAT per Unit		$13.65

Once you have this number, you will be able to better calculate the margin you will get from the average sale. Don't forget to add this onto your base cost to make each product when calculating your manufacturing costs (more on this in the next chapter). In summary, consider all aspects of shipping and logistics (which includes VAT considerations) well before you embark on your Kickstarter campaign. Do a deep dive into the shipping costs across all jurisdictions you think you will be selling into and understand the implications of VAT for your particular product. Map it all out, and then from there, you will have a better handle on how to ensure you have happy customers without making your products too expensive. In addition, you can now use these costs to set your reward tiers (or amounts you offer for the different levels detailed in chapter 9, "Ask Hurdle and Rewards").

BONUS CONTENT: Shipping

The templates in this bonus content are simply there to ensure you properly consider and calculate shipping costs and how you need to understand then apply them before you agree on how much you want to raise for your campaign.

MANUFACTURING

N THIS CHAPTER, I will work through the massive topic of manufacturing. However, I will only try and relate it specifically to how I see it effecting your Kickstarter or crowdfunding campaign. The topic of manufacturing is enormous and ever evolving. I am not going to tell you all you need to know about the topic. If I were to do that, it would be the subject of an entirely separate book. I do provide you with some recommendations in the Resources section of the website **kickstartersuccess.com,** and I also provide advisory services to others needing help in this area.

You should note also that this chapter largely relates to manufacturing of consumer electronic or fast moving consumer goods. The principles herein are sound and apply to many things that can be manufactured however if your crowdfunding campaign is for software then this chapter might not be for you.

Elaine Chen, in her book *Bringing Hardware to Market*, said, "Crowdfunding has made it possible for product teams to sell prototypes directly to backers, and these prototypes bear much less scrutiny than actual saleable products."

While that may be true, if you are ultimately building a business to sell products in the retail space, you need to understand that it does not remove your obligations to get all your official approvals and deliver a quality product.

By the end of this chapter, you will know the essential parts to and tactics for how to deal with manufacturing as it relates to your crowdfunding campaign.

If you are making a hardware product, it will most likely need to be manufactured by a third party. Many fast-moving consumer goods of an electronic nature are often manufactured in Asia, with China being one of the largest producers of these types of products.

Making a minimum viable product (MVP) or working prototype is the first step in the manufacturing process. Once you have an MVP or working prototype, you can now begin working on your manufacturing process.

There are many great online courses, books, and blogs on the process of manufacturing that you should read (such as Elaine Chen's book). However, to help you understand manufacturing in China some more, check out the resources seen on **kickstartersuccess.com** for more current links and recommendations.

If you have already asked yourself why you are going down this path and if the answer is to make loads of your product and create a business out of it, the first step you should take with your working prototype is to begin the design-for-manufacturing (DFM) process. This, put simply, is designing your product to ensure that it can easily go into mass production. If done correctly, it will assist from the manufacturing assembly perspective ensuring the most cost and time effective outcome for manufacturing.

There is much to consider behind DFM like component sourcing, selecting the right manufacturer, tooling, logo placement, packaging, drop tests, electronic interference and much, much more. However, the important thing to do is to firstly apply DFM when you start out. Most factories will do this intuitively with you, but if you are using external designers, make sure they consider the DFM process from the start. If they don't want to or think it could compromise how the product looks or feels, then they do not have your best interest at the front of mind—if you encounter this, consider looking for other designers who will.

CASE STUDY—FINDING DESIGNERS

Sadly, for us, we used a local designer who didn't really have a good handle on the manufacturing process (despite their assertion otherwise) and ended up including some serious design flaws that we could not resolve until we found a new factory.

It was with this new factory that we used DFM practices with the result being a better—much better—product for the same price.

PRO TIP Ensure your designers apply DFM principles from the start by asking your designer or factory to show you how they apply the principles

Ok, with that behind us, you are probably asking why manufacturing features as a main component for this book when the book is really about Kickstarter campaigns? Well, in my opinion, it is one of the main components that often turns a successfully funded campaign into a failure to deliver, if you get it wrong.

In any case, there are much smarter and more experienced people who have written extensively on this topic and I implore you to read blogs and books, take courses, and learn as much as you can on this topic—you can never know too much about it. Learn more from the Resources section at **www.kickstartersuccess.com**.

The systems and processes are ever changing, so don't stop researching. I think that because manufacturing has the capacity to kill your business if you make a big mistake, it is so important to understand it as best you can before jumping in. I hope to address the following topics as they relate to your crowdfunding campaign.

- Minimum order quantity
- Long lead time stock
- Approvals
- Packaging
- Payment terms

- Quality Control
- Being there (at the factory)
- Experience
- Timing
- How to navigate manufacturing

PRO TIP Research as much as possible because manufacturing is a big, big topic that you will need to have a good handle on before promising your backers anything.

MINIMUM ORDER QUANTITY (MOQ)

MOQ is the minimum amount your factory is prepared to manufacture your product. It will be different for each factory, depending on the nature of your product. The factory will have its own criteria on how they set the MOQ, which will be heavily influenced by the supply chain and their ability to negotiate within it.

Often this comes down to financial stability/credit rating of the factory within their supply chain, which often is passed on to you without your knowledge. The supply chain is where all of the components of your product are sourced from. Depending on the complexity of your product, most supply chain occurs outside of the factory you have chosen to make your product.

CASE STUDY— MOQ FROM FACTORIES

We have had MOQs from various factories of three thousand to five thousand units for Fly6 and Fly12.

Once you are through the MVP/prototyping process and (assuming it was done using the principles of DFM) you have a product that (with a few iterations) is nearly ready for mass production, you will be given a MOQ from your factory. They may have given you one when you first started with them, but it can change depending on the supply chain and availably of components.

MOQ is important as it kind of sets many things in motion for your Kickstarter campaign. I strongly recommend that you engage a factory or two and understand what MOQs you are likely to be given. This will then start informing what your minimum Kickstarter hurdle needs to be.

PRO TIP Find out as early as possible what your likely minimum order quantity is likely to be as it sets a series of cascading considerations in motion for your crowdfunding campaign.

Let's break MOQ down a little.

Imagine that your product costs US$150 (most factories in China work on a USD basis) to make and your factory says you have a MOQ of three thousand units.

If your crowdfunding campaign sells two thousand units, you still need to order the three thousand units (at a cost of US$450,000). Said another way, imagine that you are averaging a sell price on Kickstarter for your product of $250 and you have two thousand units ordered in your campaign. This means that your campaign will raise around $500,000 (yay, a success!). However, you need to factor in the cost to manufacturer the MOQ:

Cost of Minimum Order Quantity		
MOQ	Cost Per Unit	Cost to manufacturer MOQ
3000	$150	$450,000
Revenue from Crowdfunding Campaign		
Units Sold	Average selling price	Gross Revenue
2000	$250	$500,000

If you factored in the other costs it might look something like this:

Margin Analysis		
Total Amount Raised on Kickstarter		$500,000
less		
Kickstarter Fees	5%	$25,000
Payment Processing Fees	3%	$15,000
Revenue After Fees		$475,000
less		
MOQ Costs (3000 units)		$450,000
less		
Average VAT Impost*		$40,950
Cost to create campaign (per unit)		$45,000
Cost to market campaign		$60,000
Contingency		$60,000
Campaign Profit Margin / (Loss)		**($180,950)**

So now you are in the hole for $180,950, which is not a good place to be (trust me on that!).

However, you do have one thousand units in your warehouse, which in theory you can sell for between $280/unit to distributors and $499 to retail customers, which could look something like this:

Potential Revenue			
Units left after campaign	1000		
Selling Channels	Average Selling Price	% of Sales	Gross Revenue
Distributors	$280	70%	$196,000
Direct	$499	30%	$149,700
	Total Revenue		$345,700

The question would be at that point, how do you move forward owing $180,950 with only stock as your asset? It's hard to sell these units when you don't have any cash to market them. The answer is, of course, to dig in and figure out ways of selling with a shoestring budget (hustle and bootstrapping). Imagine if you could turn those remaining one thousand units into $345,700. You could pay the $180,950 you owe and have $164,750, which is around one-third of what you need to produce your next MOQ ($450,000).

Hopefully this helps you understand how important your MOQ is to your Kickstarter campaign. I talk about long lead time stock (LLTS) later. However, if you have any LLTS for your product, you often have to order and pay for it up front (before you place your first mass production run). If you are waiting for Kickstarter funds to come in to pay for LLTS, then that could delay your production runs, which then affects your delivery dates you should be promising in your campaign.

MOQ calculations should also help you set or reset your average selling prices so that you end up in a positive cash position after your campaign. This, of course, will need to be factored in against how much discount to retail price you think you need to offer to get people to pledge in the first place. Is this starting to feel like a circular equation or the chicken-or-the-egg conundrum? It should. This means all of these factors need to be iterated a number of times until you are comfortable with the intended outcome.

It's at this point that I would like to quote Blake (played by Alec Baldwin) in the movie *Glengarry Glen Ross*: "Do I have your attention?"

If this is starting to worry you somewhat, great. I've got your attention and your attention to this detail is required if you want to have a successful campaign.

To me, success in Kickstarter is delivery of products and happy customers that will invest in your products in the future. You will struggle to find your success if you are in a negative cash position! So discover your MOQ, understand how that can impact your budgets and allow for it when figuring out what price you sell your products for.

So, how do you take this info into the planning of your campaign?

Maybe you can sell more products if you drop your average selling price below $250? If you drop it to $245, will that help you sell 2,500 units? Let's work through that quickly:

$$2{,}500 \times \$245 = \$612{,}500$$

Not only have you now sold over $600,000 on Kickstarter, you have virtually broken even against your costs and now have 500 units to sell which should give you:

500 x $345 (average price from Potential Revenue table above) = $172,500

Is this a better position? I'd say yes, as you are now more likely to get deals with distributors or investors given you have shown there is more demand (by selling more units during the campaign). Even though your net position is less than the previous example, the value of more sales is that your product would now seem to be more popular.

Understanding your numbers will help guide you to success but you can't leave it until after the campaign. It must be well understood before you begin planning your campaign.

PRO TIP

Here is why MOQs are so important and how you need to know them, understand them and what they mean to you well before your campaign starts.

I'm sure everyone who starts a Kickstarter campaign hopes and thinks that they will smash it and MOQs won't matter to them. However, you will find that, even then, MOQs play an important part of the process. As I explain below, even if you sell ten thousand units on Kickstarter, and your MOQ is, say, three thousand there are still important things to consider before you place your order with your manufacturer for ten thousand units.

When you make your first batch or production run of a brand-new product, there are so many unknowns, not only for you but also for your manufacturer as well. Even if they have a vast amount of experience in your product category, every new product is unique and, thus, will require some learning from the factory. Therefore, it is very important that you should never make your first mass production run greater than the factory's set MOQ—even if you have sold many more units on Kickstarter. This is so you and the factory can test their mass production systems and the factory can learn the best way to make your product with the least amount of manufacturing issues.

If you exceed your expectations of how many units you sell on Kickstarter and this number is a multiple of the factory's set MOQ, you should place multiple MOQ orders to meet the necessary demand. Make sure each order is manufactured subsequently, not concurrently as this will make sure the factory learns from each order, improving processes and procedures, which will make each subsequent order better (from a manufacturing perspective) than the previous.

Another benefit of doing separate MOQs (particularly early in your business) is that if there are any problems specific to each order (like one of the workers was running a fever but still showed up to work but did not solder each unit the same way) can be identified and dealt with minimizing any potential brand damage. There will always—I repeat, always—be problems in the manufacturing process. It will be your job to pay attention and minimize them as they pop up.

PRO TIP Stick to MOQ size runs for the first 3-4 purchase orders, even if you sold many more multiples of the MOQ. This helps your factory learn how to reduce incidence of manufacturing errors.

LONG LEAD TIME STOCK

Depending on the components within your product and their availability in the supply chain that your manufacturer has access to, you may find that some of the components fall into the long lead time stock (LLTS) category. If this is the case, it effectively means you have to order these components in advance (of all the other components).

Sometimes LLTS is due to a genuine component supply shortage issue, and sometimes the issue is that your factory does not have the credit standing or necessary relationships with the suppliers of those components, resulting in the factory being restricted on what they can order without up-front payment. Unfortunately for you, if it is a factory credit rating issue with your manufacturer (and you won't have any visibility on this), it will fall to you and your cash flow to pay up front for the LLTS if you are to meet your desired delivery dates.

So, here you are, looking to place your first mass production order, being asked to commit to LLTS components for your products well ahead of when you need them and sometimes well before you know how many you might need. It's a tricky situation to be in because it is often well before you have the money to pay for it. Ensure that you have covered off with the manufacturer if your product is likely to have any LLTS issues, so you can factor them in to your budget and timing before you place your first order.

APPROVALS

I am assuming you are running a crowdfunding campaign that will make your products available to most of the world (subject to shipping restrictions outlined in chapter 4), and so you need to consider the fact that if you want to ship your electronic hardware product to multiple countries, you will need to seek geographically specific approvals to ensure that your product meets each local approval criteria.

"What the—?" I hear you say! Well, most electronic products need to meet various electronic emission criteria that, very loosely, mean that your products won't interfere with the communication standards of that country.

In simple terms, it means that your electronic device you are making in China won't interfere with other set electronic signals that other products like mobile phones or Wi-Fi devices use to communicate with each other.

Now you have a loose idea that there is some sort of approval you need if you want to ship your products to multiple countries. Still confused?

Let me explain: if you have a phone or other electronic device handy, have a good look at it and you should see some strange markings (usually on the back of the device) made up of letters, numbers and symbols.

These symbols are what you need to have printed somewhere on your product if you are to be allowed to sell it into various countries. To be allowed to have them on your product, you need to get your product verified by the appropriate authorities proving it meets the necessary standards. If they pass the standards, then they grant you permission to use them on your device.

CASE STUDY—APPROVALS

The cost of these approvals can range however we found that they ranged between US$2,000 and US$5,000 per approval (these costs do not include the provision of product samples that some approval agencies require for the testing and verification process).

We have had instances where the initial samples we sent in for approval did not meet their criteria and we had to re-submit more samples with additional fees, only to find the exact same product samples did meet their criteria and passed the tests the second time.

The approvals required vary depending on each product. Products with frequency emitting modules (like Bluetooth, Wi-Fi, Ant+, GPS or even just electrical power) will definitely require such approvals. Your factory will know what is required early on during the manufacturing process and should be able to give you an in-order-of-cost quote to apply for them.

Sometimes these approvals can take months to achieve so factor that into your campaign timing. You can't put the marks on your devices without approval from the governing authorities, and you can't legally ship them into the country without the approval. You need to have your factory starting the approval process early. Discuss this topic with your factory in your initial discussions so it can be factored into your delivery promise to your backers.

PACKAGING

You may think that your device is the most complicated thing you have to make. However, packaging can involve a number of design factors that can boggle the mind.

Will your product be sold in shops? It might need a hang tab. You might not think that your precious product will be dropped by careless shop assistants or clumsy shoppers, but that does not matter because you need to design your packaging so that it can withstand a series of drop tests. So, suddenly it needs to be more robust than just bubble wrapped in a mailer bag!

PRO TIP Know your profit margins before deciding where you are going to sell your product so you can set your pricing correctly.

Is your product only proposed to be sold via Amazon? Then you should design your packaging specifically to minimize costs and weight. Think through the sales process:

1. Your customer views the images on your Amazon product page.

2. They make a decision on the product images and description, not the packaging

3. They pay for the product before receiving it, so you don't need to worry so much about the packaging (your packaging is an important part of your customers' experience with your brand, so you might still want them to have a great experience, but just weigh that against the cost of packaging and how that affects your bottom line).

PRO TIP Understand where (retail, direct or Amazon) you are going to be selling your product before designing the packaging.

PAYMENT TERMS

There is a saying that everything is negotiable, and I'm sure there are books written on the subject matter.

The conditions which you have agreed to pay for your products are called terms. This will include how much deposit to pay, when you pay the balance, what currency the payment is to be made in, and where (geographically speaking) the products are to have the ownership transferred. These are just some examples.

Your factory will have standard terms that they work on, and you need to find these out early to see if they are going to meet your needs or if they can be negotiated to better suit your situation. Negotiating terms with your manufacturer is an important factor in making sure your business can manage its finances effectively to give it the best chance of success. There are many questions that need to be raised and here are some to consider asking:

- How much is the deposit?

- When do they want the balance?

- Can you use payment factoring to extend when the balance is due and what are the additional costs?

- What currency do you pay in?

- Where (geographically) does the ownership transfer for the goods?

- What are the insurance provisions?

- What are the warranty provisions?

- How do we (it's a joint effort) deal with returns?

CASE STUDY—DEPOSITS TO FACTORIES

We found that every new factory we used always wanted a substantial deposit before they started manufacturing our products. These terms were relaxed when the factory had done a couple of production runs with us once we had proved we would pay the invoices in full and on time.

Can you negotiate the terms with your factory?

If you can work through those questions and achieve favorable terms, this will help your business enormously. For example, if you can pay your factory thirty or sixty days after you have taken receipt of your products, this will minimize your cost of capital dramatically, especially if you are managing to sell your products quickly.

If you have to pay for your products in full before you take possession of them (which is common for first-time manufacturing runs as you establish your relationship with the factory), this will mean you need to have all of your funds locked away before you place your first mass production order. Orders placed with your factory are called purchase orders (POs).

Even if you have negotiated some deferred payment terms with your factory, the management of your limited funds can be a real challenge because often there are so many other things you need to spend money on. If you don't set aside the full amount for your first PO, you can fall short of working capital before it comes time to pay the balance of the PO. This problem does not go away even if you do a multimillion-dollar crowdfunding campaign. The solution is to set aside all the funds required to pay for your PO as soon as they become available and find working capital (money) from somewhere else.

PRO TIP Amongst the first questions you put to prospective manufacturers should be, what terms do you offer?

QUALITY CONTROL (QC)

This is one of those topics that seem to be top of mind as people often ask me, "how do you manage quality control in China?" We had to learn the hard way with quality control when we first started, we were very inexperienced in manufacturing and relied heavily on our local designers and their relationships with a single factory. What we found, unfortunately, was our local designers actually had little idea on design-for-manufacturing principles and just relied on their factory to work through the design issues of our product. We had never explained our product to the factory, so they were working in a vacuum. This led to many design flaws in our first product, but more on that later.

You might think that any factory would be happy to take a new product on board, and this could be proved by most factories you talk to saying 'yes' to whatever you want to make with them. However, each factory you work with on a new product takes on some of the risk. The risk of it working in the field, the risk that you will be able to pay for POs, the risk that you only place one PO and never order again are common risks that they have to consider.

PRO TIP Find a factory that sells products into the same regions that you want to sell in. If you want to sell into retail in the United States, make sure the factory you select also makes products that sell into that region. Go out and buy them and test them to see if the quality standards are similar to yours, and if so, then you can confidently begin negotiations with them.

CASE STUDY—MANAGING QUALITY FROM CHINA

What we found on the manufacturing side was that our original factory didn't really care much about quality control.

As it happened, we went to China to attend the very first production run of our first product, Fly6, and found that over 35 percent of the units that rolled off the production line did not even power on.

We were mortified because we had previously manufactured two pilot production runs of two hundred units each that were flawless. In fact, I still see some of those original units on bikes today some five or six years later. So, you can imagine that our expectations of the very next production run of three thousand units to be exactly the same.

How wrong we were. We were quite alarmed by what we saw and were very concerned that the factory owner was simply saying to us, "Don't worry about it. I will just replace any product that doesn't work." What he couldn't seem to understand was that our customers would not find it acceptable. More than that, we did not find it acceptable!

To resolve this problem, we ended up hiring a local person to work full time for us at the factory. Her job was to physically check and test each product as it came off the production line. We trained her to observe all details, test each function of the products, and if there were any deviation from our standards, give it back to the factory owner to fix it up.

This is how we managed a bad situation to make sure that each of our first customers (our Kickstarter backers) would get a working product. At the same time, we realized that this factory was not a viable option for us if we wanted to create good products for our customers. It was after we trained up our new quality control team member that we started looking for a new factory.

The lesson here is that your factory must understand that you are selling products where it is very important to each customer to have a good experience with the product they have just bought from you. If they have a good experience (the product just works), then they are more likely to recommend it to their friends, which, in turn, will create more orders which the factory can then make more money from.

We went on to interview six new factories, the first five of which said yes to every question we had. We felt like they were just saying that to win our business. Each had some experience in electronic goods, ranging from bike lights to female pleasure devices! The last factory we met with seemed to have the best experience. However, what impressed us the most was that it felt as though they were interviewing us to see if we would be a fit for them. To us, this meant they were concerned with building a sustainable working relationship.

Another factor that appealed to us from this last factory was that they were supplying products that were predominantly sold in the United States. This was music to our ears, as it told us that they had their quality control under control! This factory was concerned about not only quality but also our ability to successfully run our business. They wanted to know if we had a business plan and if we had a product roadmap. They were basically checking to see if we were a viable business for them to take on as a new client.

This gave us a great deal of confidence in this factory that we could work with them to make good quality products well into the future. This factory ended up making over fifty thousand units for us.

After our bad experience with the first factory, we managed the design process more carefully. We also hired third-party quality control companies who were trained to spot any issues after the units were made and before they left the factory. This process adds a few extra days and some expense to the process but is really essential. Check out the Resources section of **kickstartersuccess.com** to see who I recommend you should use for quality control on your products if you are making them in China.

BEING THERE

Maybe you have all your manufacturing systems in place and can make your product remotely without any problems. However, during your Kickstarter campaign, there is nothing that lets your audience know you are on top of your game

CASE STUDY—ATTENDING THE FACTORY

We found that having direct communication with the factory versus via a design firm or intermediary was much more effective. If I look back now, moving to direct communication with the factory actually saved our business.

We were getting frustrated with our designers, who were controlling the flow of information from the factory. We were not getting timely information and when eventually we did get information, it was often wrong or out of date. We soon learned the only way to make sure the factory was getting the correct information was to talk directly to them.

I remember very early in the design stage of Fly6 when we provided the design specifications to the designers of which one specification was to have the video output in MP4 format as opposed to AVI format. When we got our first working prototype, we looked at the files in the directory, and they had the .MP4 file listing. We thought, "Great!"

What we didn't know was that the file type was actually AVI, but they hard coded the software to rewrite the extension to MP4. We figured this out when we found normal video players that normally worked with MP4 files would not play the video.

This was a major issue we would not overcome for some years simply because the factory said they would only use a particular supplier (a microprocessor brand that was not compatible with MP4), which meant we could only ever have AVI format.

This was a massive disappointment for us as we knew our customers wanted MP4 format. It highlighted how little our designers (who were also our project managers at that point) knew of what was happening. This led us to take on the project management and attend the factory more often to manage these and other issues as they came up.

better than sharing factory visits with your backers. Not only does it show your backers how things are progressing on your project but also it helps you bring them along your journey with you.

A few choice photos or videos of you with the tooling, factory workers, or components are all that's needed. Most of your backers have never been to China or elsewhere in Asia and could be very interested to see the mechanics behind the manufacturing process.

In my experience, you can achieve so much more productivity when you are there at the factory than you can over Skype, phone, or email.

Go there and get stuck into the grit of the whole manufacturing process. You will find improvements for your product you would never have otherwise found. For around US$1,000, you can fly from Los Angles to Hong Kong and get some accommodation near your factory (if located in Shenzhen). The benefits you will get will outweigh the cost by a substantial multiple. Do it—be there!

Here is a photo taken during one of our visits to the factory during our first Kickstarter campaign:

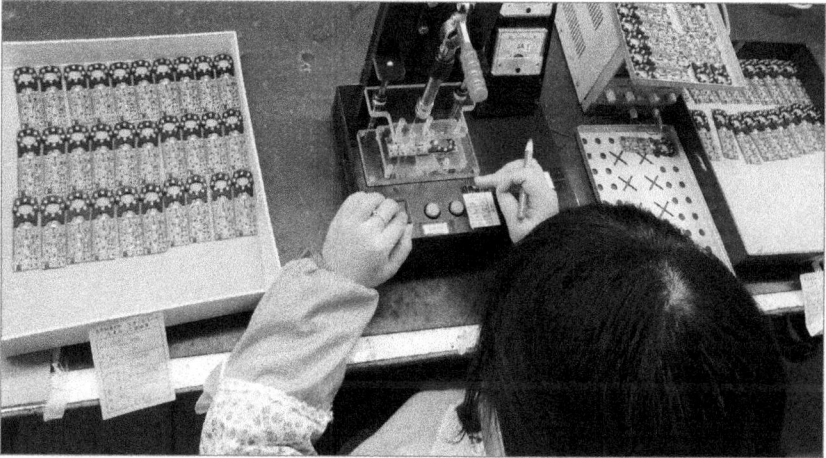

As touched on, communicating with your factory can take many forms, but we found there is no substitute for your time spent in the factory with the factory owner or your product manager. We seemed to be able to achieve about two months' worth of remote work in just four to five days on-site on the factory floor. It can be a lot of fun, too!

CASE STUDY—FINDING A GOOD MANUFACTURER

Our second factory was already making camera products and knew some of the intrinsic risks with our type of product so that when they took it on board, they priced it appropriately and knew what they were getting into.

From our perspective, we had the confidence that they made products for our largest target market (United States). It is this demographic that would demand good quality, which is what we wanted to deliver to our customers. Confidence in your manufacturer is what you want to have —seek it out, and when you find it, nurture it as if it is the only one you will ever find.

We knew in the first meeting with them that they would be a good fit for us. As they had experience in a similar product, they identified in the first meeting some of the failings in our existing product that proved correct.

They took our original product, improved the design, the camera, the battery and reduced its size while giving longer battery life. They delivered a working prototype in less than four weeks. This was a game changer for our business and proves how important a good manufacturing partner can be.

Here is the change the new factory made in less than four weeks. Smaller, better quality, longer lasting and more. Old unit on the right, new on the left.

EXPERIENCE

How much experience does your factory have in the product space you are hoping to sell your product in? This can play a large part in how effective they can be for the manufacturing of your product. If they have no experience in the product segment you are in (like our first factory when we made Fy6), there are several risks you need to be aware of.

They can underquote you to manufacture the products, giving you a false sense of financial understanding of what you are about to undertake.

Imagine if they quoted you $30/unit for your product and you based your Kickstarter campaign on this. Then when you are ready to do your first mass production run, they then give you a formal quote, saying it actually is going to be $50 per unit. This could sink your campaign in an instant and is why I suspect some infamous Kickstarter campaigns fail.

We felt that our factory was learning how to manufacture our product by making all the mistakes. I can absolutely say that this is what happened with us on our first factory. In hindsight, I wished we had done more research on who was making our products to ensure they already had some base level experience.

After we moved to a new factory, the one we just left could then go on to advertise to other prospective clients that they had experience in camera products for the worldwide market. That's great for them, but we would have effectively paid for it by the factory making their mistakes at our cost.

Our second factory could clearly demonstrate their experience in the camera electronic consumer market. This gave us much more confidence they could achieve all the important things for us like development time frames, cost management, and most importantly, quality.

One of the things that resonated deeply with us with our second factory was how our main factory contact (project manager) was well traveled and attended all the current electronic shows around the world. It provided him with a high level of market understanding from the factory side of what our customer base was after.

Many times, have we heard the "yes, yes, yes" of Chinese suppliers when asked to deliver a certain aspect when they really don't know what our customers want. This well-traveled staff member displayed a solid understanding of what our customers want and proved himself invaluable to us.

CASE STUDY– SELECTING FACTORIES WITH INTEGRITY

A caveat here is that we did meet some factories that had experience in electronic goods in the same industry as we were in, but when we visited their factories, they seemed to be happy to show us all the inner workings of other products they were making for their other clients.

They even offered us samples of these products! This was quite a concern as it probably meant that if we manufactured our products with them, they would similarly allow our competitors to take samples of our products, too.

This security issue was highlighted when we were asked to wait in an office while they gathered the people for the meeting and in that office was a sample of a competitor's product that had not yet been released to the public. This was enough of an issue for us that we resolved to not even consider using this factory for our products.

The factory we ultimately settled on also showed us through their factory. This factory, in comparison to the others we had toured, was clean and orderly. We asked if we could take photos, but they did not allow it. This impressed us and highlighted to us that they had integrity for their clients. It was another reason we chose them to work with us.

TIMING

Through your Kickstarter campaign, you would have promised your backers when you would be delivering them their reward.

When you can deliver on this promise will be largely tied to your manufacturer who, before you start your Kickstarter campaign, should have given you some sort of timeline as to when your "goodies" would be ready for shipping.

As mentioned above, there are many factors that affect timing and you need to be all over them but try—try!—to understand that not everything goes to plan in manufacturing. You should allow some wriggle room when you set up your time lines. This not only protects your brand or personal integrity by giving you more chance to deliver on time, but also is better for your backers.

They know that what you are doing is difficult (otherwise they would be doing it themselves) and that not every Kickstarter project is delivered on time, so give yourself that extra time in your program and tell them that you are going to give it your best to deliver on time but add a couple of months onto your time-line if you are making a hardware product.

Kickstarter statistics tell us that overall only 35 percent of campaigns are successful and, worst yet, less than 20 percent of technology projects reached their target, but the statistics don't have any visibility on how many projects actually deliver on time. My guess is, it would be less than 5 percent. We were very proud to deliver our Fly6 products in the month we estimated in the campaign and to us that was the ultimate success!

Hopefully, you can get a flavor of how critically important manufacturing is to your campaign and that there are a multitude of factors within manufacturing that you need to consider before you start planning your campaign. Don't forget to sign up for some current courses to deep dive into these and other topics listed in the Resources section of **kickstartersuccess.com**.

HOW TO NAVIGATE MANUFACTURING

Manufacturing, as you have just read, is no simple topic to master and is also full of risks. Other than questions about Kickstarter, it's one of the most common questions I get asked: how can you make stuff in China?

As it is something I love to work on, I also help companies build up their capabilities to manufacture in China using my experience and connections, which are ideally suited to crowdfunding projects. It's an amazing feeling to take an idea from your head and see it as a fully packaged consumer product on the shelf of a store. Feel free to reach out to me at **kickstartersuccess.com** if you are looking for help on your campaign.

BONUS CONTENT: Manufacturing Checklist

This checklist is by no means exhaustive as each product will have its own specific details. However, it will ensure you have covered off the essential and high-level issues with your manufacturer, so you don't make the same mistakes we did!

PRODUCT SAMPLES

N THIS CHAPTER, you will understand the importance of creating samples over and above what you would normally need for product development. In addition, you will see firsthand how effective the use of product samples is in creating some of the best media coverage for your project. More specifics on how this relates to marketing your product are covered in chapter 10, "Marketing." I hope that by the end of this chapter you will use this information to preplan and budget for additional samples when everyone else will be telling you not to.

The provision of samples to notable persons (people or publications with extensive reach) in your target market/industry is a very powerful tool. With our most important media relating to cycling and sports tech, we asked if they would like to join us in the prototyping and product development journey, and those who accepted were asked to keep all information embargoed until an agreed time (usually at the launch of the Kickstarter campaign).

They basically got access to physical prototypes and firmware upgrades as we developed them. With some of the media (an even more select group), we also allowed them to be the first to provide their reviews. This exclusivity was often traded for a more comprehensive or in-depth review so there was a win-win outcome.

The benefit of providing samples to these key influencers, even though each sample costs a significant amount of money, was that the person doing the review or story was not just regurgitating a media release with a limited selection of images (that all media usually has access to); they were personally using the product for a time leading up to the Kickstarter campaign and taking their own photos or making their own videos and providing their own personal opinions.

When the public reads these types of reviews or stories, they will see how much more genuine they are, and this flows through to building your credibility over and above the typical media releases. You would have seen them if you have done some research—"as seen in blah blah blah"—where almost every story is a carbon copy of your media release and stock images.

Below is a screen shot from a piece *Wired* magazine did using one of our prototypes we provided to them.

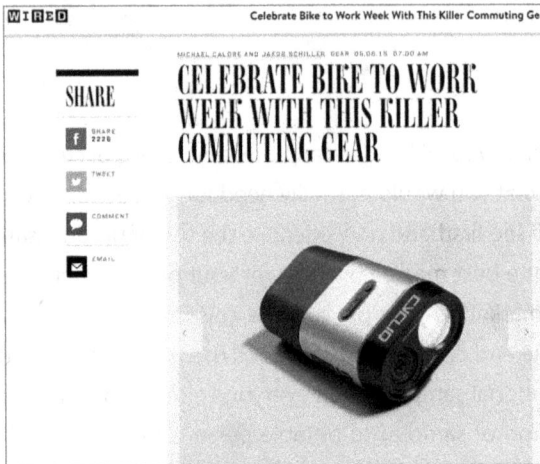

Image courtesy of Wired *magazine*
(https://www.wired.com/2015/05/bike-to-work-gear/)

How many samples to make is a difficult decision and will depend on your product, the market, how many influencers you are targeting, and many more factors.

This feedback process is mostly to help us improve the product for the manufacturing process. However, we found it useful to have the personal accounts for the Kickstarter campaign where you can see we provided some sample quotes from some of the people testing the products. Luckily for us, one of the most well-known personalities in professional cycling and commentating, Phil Liggett, was one of the persons who agreed to test our product for us, and he loved it. It helps that your product works as promised as these people are not going to lie about their experiences and have it promoted publicly.

CASE STUDY—USING PRODUCT SAMPLES & GETTING FEEDBACK

With Fly6, we made four hundred samples, as we wanted to get as much feedback as possible and have plenty of samples for media. We found that when people were asked to test a free sample and provide regular feedback, 95 percent of them took the sample but hardly provided useful feedback, even when prompted (many times). This was pretty disappointing for us given the expense and effort gone into providing it to them. However, we learned our lesson.

Future samples and testing was provided to twenty well-known testers that provided valuable feedback and twenty samples for media. This was more than enough feedback as it included different countries, different weather conditions, different cycling types, and most importantly, different people.

This quote (below) from *Wired* magazine actually says that all the gear in the piece has been road tested by Wired staffers and earns their recommendation. Validating the importance of getting something physical in the hands of influencers or your target media.

> TWO-WHEELERS TAKE NOTE: May 11-15 is National Bike to Work Week. Of course, for many of us, every week is Bike to Work week. But the good people at the League of American Bicyclists have put this awareness campaign together to sway the merely bike-curious. In fact, the entire month of May is stacked with events to encourage cycling. It's the best time of year to explore the loveliest of commuting options: the weather is agreeable, the daylight hours are plenty, and road safety is strengthened by a larger number of cyclists. What we've gathered here is a collection of essentials, outwear, and tools to serve you on your daily bike commute. All of this gear has been road-tested by WIRED staffers over the last few months, and all of it earns our recommendation. With these picks, all you need is a bike and you're ready to go make that bacon.

CASE STUDY—HAVING WORKING SAMPLES

Perhaps the most important thing that came out of having working samples in the world is that you get to have real-life-use cases that you can showcase to backers proving that your products do "as it says on the box!"

Both Paul Ludlow and Craige (surname withheld) had terrible incidents while riding their bikes. However, using our products they were able to have the offenders prosecuted, and their insurance paid up in full for medical and physical damage.

Below are some of the quotes from cyclists using our Fly6 product used in our Fly12 campaign to validate our concept and prove that our products actually worked. It was a great help that Phil Liggett, a famous Tour de France commentator and journalist liked our product so much that he offered his quote.

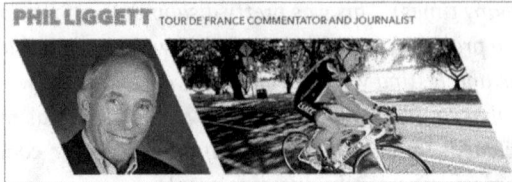

PHIL LIGGETT TOUR DE FRANCE COMMENTATOR AND JOURNALIST

I thought the Fly6 was the best thing to happen to promote safer cycling and now it is set to pair up with Fly12. The Fly6 is a must have on our busy roads and the images it produces are amazing. Can't recommend it highly enough to everyone.

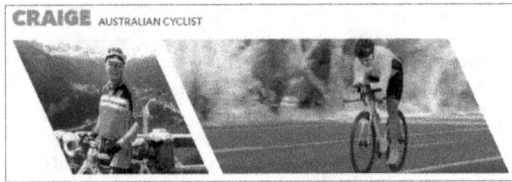

CRAIGE AUSTRALIAN CYCLIST

Like all cyclists, I am concerned about my safety when I am on the road. The Fly6 didn't stop my accident from happening, but it did provide the evidence to police and the insurance company that showed the driver was clearly negligent when two of my mates and I were hit from behind by a car traveling at 80kph.

PAUL LUDLOW AUSTRALIAN CYCLIST

I had a very bad accident on my bike as I was hit by a car while commuting, but my Fly6 recorded the whole event and instead of me paying thousands of dollars, the police saw the footage, charged the driver and his insurance covered all my expenses. I never ride without my Fly6 and soon with Fly12.

BONUS CONTENT: Product Sample Tracking Sheet

The bonus content for this chapter is a sample tracking sheet that you can use to manage how you work with your influencers and samples you have sent them.

YOUR PROTOTYPE

WHILE THIS CHAPTER IS BRIEF, it highlights something very important that you need to know many months ahead of doing a hardware-based Kickstarter campaign. You will, at the end of the chapter, know this important information which will ensure you don't "false start."

In theory, you should already have a working prototype if you are thinking of doing a Kickstarter campaign. However, it's a little-known fact that the good folks at Kickstarter HQ won't let you proceed with a hardware campaign unless you can prove to them that you have a working prototype of your product. This is a good thing for all as it makes sure that your concept is real, which is the first hurdle you have to overcome if you eventually want to make a business out of your idea.

You can't launch on Kickstarter without a verifiable working prototype, so start there!

PRO TIP

For Kickstarter, this hurdle makes sure that the campaigns on their platform are not spurious. Otherwise, they would get random ideas that could not possibly become real, meaning any campaign that achieves its funding target will likely not deliver, leaving backers disillusioned with the process. This is a good thing for both backers and the whole crowdfunding ecosystem—keep it up, Kickstarter!

Rendered realistic images do not count, nor do videos showing the products working when they are computer generated. Sometimes the Kickstarter staff will ask for a physical sample or sometimes you can do a Skype chat with them to show them you have an actual working prototype. Sometimes, your campaign and video will prove that you obviously have a working prototype. It would just depend on your product and the Kickstarter staff assigned to assess it.

The whole principle is that you have got your idea working and are looking for backers on the crowdfunding platform to help you refine and mass-produce it—not invent it!

The message here is simple: if you think you need three or four months to build a working prototype, don't plan on starting a Kickstarter campaign beforehand!

CASE STUDY—FLY12 PROTOTYPES

With our Fly12 prototypes, we also went to the trouble of designing cost effective and grungy packaging so that when we sent the prototypes to our influencers and testers, they had an awesome-looking prototype delivered to their door that showed we cared about them and the process they were undertaking for us. It was totally unnecessary given it was just a prototype, but we felt it was a nice touch for our influences and testers.

Left is prototyping packaging and right is retail packaging for the original Fly12 model.

BONUS CONTENT: How Prototypes Drive Campaign Timing

In the bonus content is a Gantt chart template that you can use to track some of the major tasks with getting your prototypes finished and that affects your Kickstarter campaign timing.

LISTS AND DATABASES

I N THIS CHAPTER, you will learn how important your database is and how to effectively use it to build the hype and demand leading up to your campaign launch. I provide an example on how you can use this from one month out from your campaign launch.

Your database (list) is one of your most valuable things in relation to getting backers to pledge for your project. In theory, every time you use the list, it should generate revenue or the potential for revenue. Given its importance, you should be looking to grow the list at every opportunity.

A tactic you can use to build your database is, if you have a website, offer a competition that targets your potential customers and ask for email addresses to enter the competition. Be creative, be bold, but always be genuine to your ideal potential customer—this will help make the list more valuable per entry.

For example, imagine you are selling a new type of surfboard. Do not target people that live five hours drive from the ocean. If you did, when you use the list to sell your products, you will get less utility out of it because those people don't have any surf near them and probably wouldn't want one. Focus your list on your ideal potential customer, and you will find that each time you use the list you will generate more revenue per database entry.

You will find you are inundated with companies and people selling you "qualified"(cough, cough) lists of potential backers. My advice is that if you are even considering using one of the lists, take the amount you were proposing to spend on it and do a targeted Facebook campaign. This should yield you more backers every time.

Don't buy lists unless they are qualified and very specific to your target market, and even then, there is always the law of diminishing returns with the age of a list. The problem with these offers is that you can never tell how well qualified the list is because you never see it. If you do some research on this topic, you will see some people have posted their results after using these list-sellers services without any spike in sales. This was the same with our first campaign where we paid seven hundred dollars to have our campaign "blasted out" to a qualified database, but we did not get any discernible spike in backers.

Now, that is easy to say, as my campaigns are over, and when you are doing a campaign, you are always looking for ways to get your campaign in front of new eyeballs. So I understand the temptation to use these tantalizing offers. My advice to you if you really are considering using them is to use a performance-based deal with the person selling it to you. If they don't want to do that, then you know it is not worthwhile.

I call this method: Bullshit-Based Performance Metrics (BBPM). Use the template below in response to these people trying to sell you lists using BBPM. It will help you manage these requests effectively and with a bit of fun! My guess is that none will respond proving the real worth of their offering—zero.

BBPM Template

Hi (insert name here),

Thanks so much for your offer to use your database to promote my campaign to your list of qualified persons.

I would love to take you up on your offer.

To start with, I will pay you 10 percent of your total fee and ask that you send my campaign to 10 percent of your database. This will no doubt show a spike in sales (because your list is so good and contains well-qualified backers). On the basis that I can see a discernible spike in backers, I'd like to propose the following:

Next, I pay you 20 percent of your total fee for you to send my campaign out to another 20 percent of your database. On the basis that I see a doubling in sales compared to the first time, I will be very happy to pay the balance 70 percent of your fee to send my campaign out to the balance of your list.

Yours sincerely,
Campaign Creator

ASK HURDLE AND REWARDS

ASK HURDLE

Ask hurdle is the amount of funding you set to be your minimum amount raised on your Kickstarter campaign. Setting this target (or hurdle) is a very challenging process that requires a considerable amount of deep thought. If you get this very wrong on Kickstarter, you might not get funded.

Setting your ask hurdle involves a mixture of science and psychology. The science of it is that you need enough money to get the job done (delivering your products to your backers). The psychology of it is that only you and your team really know what it is going to cost to achieve your goal, so it almost does not matter what the number that you set for your campaign is. However, you need to convey to the backers that the ask hurdle, once achieved, will enable you to deliver what they have pledged for. In addition, you need to set a number that you think you can achieve as well as trying to fit within the reasonable parameters that other campaigns in your category or of similar nature have achieved.

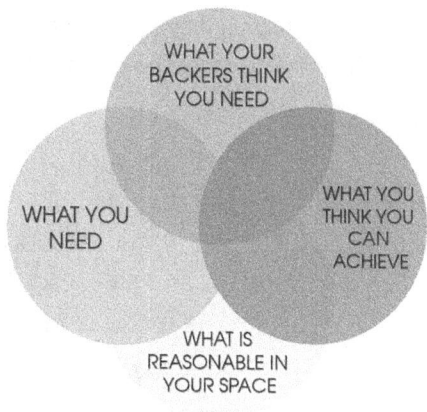

WHAT YOUR BACKERS THINK YOU NEED

WHAT YOU NEED

WHAT YOU THINK YOU CAN ACHIEVE

WHAT IS REASONABLE IN YOUR SPACE

Where these four factors meet should be where you should begin your consideration of what your ask hurdle should be. Let's explore what each circle means:

What you need—this is the cash you think you need based on your budget to get the goods delivered to the backers (your minimum in this case should most likely be based on the MOQ given to you by the factory and your maximum should not be too far from this point). There should be science behind this number!

What backers think you need—this will be based on how you portray the campaign, loosely based on how prepared or ready you are to start production of your product. If you are in a position to start production ASAP, then the amount should be lower, and if you are just starting out, it will need to be higher. The goal here is to give the backer the belief that the ask hurdle will be enough for you to get the job done—most definitely in the psychology realm!

What you think you can achieve—This should be based on your research on other campaigns and your belief that your offering is going to be 'so much better' than others. A mixture of science and psychology.

What is reasonable in your space—this should be totally based on your research on other crowdfunding campaigns for similar offerings and how much they raised. I can't say enough about looking at similar campaigns, deconstructing them, and trying to understand what works and what doesn't. This research should be ever present when building your campaign!

PRO TIP Start your hurdle discussion by drawing a Venn diagram of four circles. 1) What amount you need. 2) What the backers think you need 3) What you think you can achieve 4) What is reasonable in your space. Where they meet is where you should start.

REWARDS

There are many reasons why addressing rewards with careful consideration is important. However, I want to focus on the fact that, no matter how set you initially feel you are set with your reward tiers, you will find you need to revisit them several times, adjusting the value before you launch your campaign.

PRO TIP Kick around your first thoughts on the reward levels, but know that they will and should change many times before you launch the campaign. Once live, you cannot change them.

First thing is first—why are you doing the campaign? Is it to make profit? Is it to raise awareness of your brand? Is it to sell as many units as possible or is it to hit some dollar-value target? Each one of these potential reasons could lead you to structure your reward tiers very differently.

Let's look at turning a profit from your campaign. If this is your ultimate or most important reason for doing a Kickstarter campaign, then you need to know or learn very quickly exactly what all of your costs are (refer to chapter 5, "Manufacturing"). This will help you set your cost base for the campaign (which is the total costs you will incur making your crowdfunding campaign).

CASE STUDY– WORKING THROUGH REWARD TIERS

With our third campaign, we had our first meeting to address rewards tiers, knowing that we would revise them a number of times before launch, so the first session could focus on all the necessary principles as opposed to getting all the reward tiers correct.

For most Kickstarter campaigns, one of your reward tiers will be your most popular with your backers. This is most likely where you will raise the most funds. Out of all the reward tiers you set, you have to try to make this one have some healthy profit built in. Let me explain:

Using our example, this product costs $150 to make even though you are proposing to sell it in the shops for $499. This reward tier needs to be a great deal for the backers, and if it is, it will become your most popular reward tier.

So, what does 'great deal' mean?

This means something different for everyone. However, it seems to be 30–50 percent off your final or retail price. Using our example, this tier would be between $290–$310, depending on a bunch of things—like whether there are others doing a similar product on Kickstarter or available in retail already and you "need" to smash them on price, or previous Kickstarter campaigns with a similar product pricing that did or didn't work.

If your primary goal is to make profit, then you can't sell this average or most popular tier at $160, given your costs are $150. You need to factor in your margin and then estimate how much you want to make. If you think that you could sell 500–1000 units (or more) at this tier, and your average tier level gave you $30 of profit margin per unit, you will likely be making between $15,000–$30,000 profit for your whole campaign.

This is on the basis that your early bird rewards will cost you money or break even and your higher tier rewards will make you more money per unit; the average will generally be at your most popular tier. If the amount of profit at this most popular reward tier is not enough for you, then you need to set the average tier at a higher amount.

However, you have to understand that people, in general, are price sensitive, and Kickstarter backers are even more so—they are hunting for a bargain, and if your main reward tier is too close to the final retail price, it's likely they will move on to the next campaign and wait for the product to hit the retail shelf and buy it then (with the return policy and warranties included).

If your goal is to sell as many as possible and make your profit on volume, then you need to plan your rewards to allow for a very small margin on each item and place your tiers very close together. you might think of pricing them like this:

Reward Levels				
Tier	Pledge	Limit	RRP	Discount
Super Super early bird	199	100	499	60%
Super early bird	219	200	499	56%
Early Bird	239	400	499	52%
Crazy Deal	249	unlimited	499	50%
Twin Pack	460	200	998	54%

Of course, your product might suit other tiers (doubles, team deals, multiples, etc.), but They can follow the same principle. If you are chasing more profit per tier, simply increase the pledge amount of each tier without moving out of what I feel is the sweet spot of between 30 and 50 percent off the RRP.

The other important consideration is to try and make the tiers simple as possible. Too many or confusing tiers make it hard for backers to make a choice. The goal here is to make it as easy as possible for your backers to understand, make a choice, and click the green pledge button. "Less is more" should be the guiding principle when it comes to reward tiers.

In many ways, this should be looked at as part of the sales funnel and the last part of the funnel before the transaction takes place. Make it simple; make it compelling.

Simple reward tiers creates a compelling call to action. Keep them simple.

PRO TIP

I note there is some current discussion online about the efficacy or virtue of early bird pledge levels, and while some of the discussion is very valid, I can only talk for how it worked successfully for our campaigns. I fully recommend them!

CASE STUDY—EARLY BIRD TIERS

I felt our tier rewards, and in particular, our early bird rewards, were a strong driver for the superfast path to hitting our funding hurdles, which then led on to getting issues with a staff pick badge from the Kickstarter staff, nearly funded, featured, and what's popular Kickstarter lists, which then lead to even more people seeing and backing our projects.

This was success building on success. The proof was in our last two campaigns, where we hit our hurdle in 2.5 hours, which got us listed in those important Kickstarter lists. I truly feel that the early bird tier system was the key driver in this regard.

BONUS CONTENT: Reward Level Sheet

This template will help you set out your reward tiers. Don't forget that the numbers will change many times before you launch your campaign but use this template to track them as you go.

MARKETING

I N THIS CHAPTER, I work through what I think is the single best form of marketing you can do for a Kickstarter campaign and how I used it. This tactic effectively marketed our products to give our fans a genuine and authentic reason to pledge toward our campaigns, raising over $1,000,000.

❝ Always be closing. ❞

This line was delivered by Alec Baldwin as the character Blake in the movie *Glengarry Glen* Ross. Given this is my second quote from this movie, you can probably tell that I love this movie—particularly an awesome scene I recommend you watch where Blake gives an intense sales speech to a bunch of real estate salesmen. The message was as simple as ABC—Always Be Closing, or in other words, Always Be Selling. It's something as a founder you have to take onboard and burn into your character.

Whatever it is you are making, you should always be selling it to everyone you meet.

- You are selling the benefits it is going to deliver to people who are going to buy it.

- You are selling why it is a good investment to investors.

- You are selling why people should risk their pledge to you during your campaign.

- You are selling the reasons why the company you have hired to produce your Kickstarter video would benefit by discounting their normal rates to help you with your campaign.

- You are selling the excitement of your project to potential cofounders, staff, consultants, or advisors.

What is the message? You should always be selling. To me, marketing is selling, and you should always be marketing.

There are many forms of marketing available, and over time, different forms have different levels of success. In terms of paid marketing, Facebook has consistently been the best return on investment (ROI) for our campaigns. Almost all marketing experts will be able to help you manage your Facebook marketing campaigns around your Kickstarter project, so I won't go into detail on this aspect.

I'd like to focus on what I feel is the best form of marketing. It's called validation. You will find that endorsement of a product by someone that you know or trust is a very powerful purchasing suggestion.

Giving your products to influencers is a great way of reaching an audience with some level of validation. However, its effectiveness does vary widely depending on what type of influencer they are. With celebrity influencers, I feel that everyone knows they get paid to validate a product—which, in my opinion, dramatically diminishes the value of the endorsement.

The most effective endorsements that I have used are ones that are genuine, and this can only happen when someone is using your product for what it was designed for. How then, you might ask, do you get your product (which might only be in prototype form) into the hands of genuine influencers? It's actually quite simple, although not necessarily easy.

The best way, which should work with almost any type of product (hardware- or software-based) is to select the most influential person or outlet (like a magazine or blog) and ask if they would like to join you on your journey to develop your product.

In most cases you will not yet know this person or company personally, but you will need to ask them to use your product. This would likely mean you have to share certain trade secrets with them or market-sensitive information that is embedded in your product. This, in turn, means you will have to trust that they will hold your secret information under embargo until an agreed time. Embargo in this case means holding back information until an agreed time. With our campaigns, the agreed-upon time was often the launch day for each campaign.

There is always a risk that this person or group you are inviting into your inner circle might leak some vital information about your product to get some sort of first-mover advantage. The good thing is that most people understand the long game in media, and that is to keep their word and manage your sensitive information carefully.

If they manage your information carefully this time for you, it's likely they will get opportunities again and again, giving them a better long-term advantage. In my experience, the media and personalities we tapped into were all very sensitive to our intellectual property.

CASE STUDY—FINDING INFLUENCERS

So, how can this work practically? Let me describe using Fly6 as an example. Fly6 is a HD camera & light for cyclists, so it fits into the sports tech hardware category as a retail product. Or you could say it is in the following categories: sports, tech, start-up, innovation, safety, action camera, and cycling. When considering who would be the best influencers, I researched bloggers, vloggers, reviewers, and magazines in those categories to try and find who I thought would be the best fit.

Luckily for our product genre, there is one go-to person in the industry who is the most widely respected blogger/reviewer in sports tech: DC Rainmaker, or DCR (dcrainmaker.com). The man behind the blog is Ray Maker, who provides the most comprehensive and honest reviews of the latest sports tech gadgets.

If you are considering buying any sports tech, check out his site for the best in-depth reviews. What makes DCR so good? It's his complete honesty and detailed reviews. Large company or small, if Ray finds flaws, inconsistencies, or thinks your product does not do what it says on the box, he is going to reveal it, call you out on it, and give his unbiased and raw opinion on it. I'm pretty sure this is what his readers love about his reviews.

So DCR is clearly the industry guru in the sports tech field, and a good review from him is a valuable endorsement. But equally, if your product is crap, he is going to call you out on it to all your potential customers—so be prepared for the real deal to get published. With Fly6, we knew we had a good concept that addressed the safety needs for cyclists that had never been addressed before, but we didn't really know if we could execute the development and manufacturing of it well enough to meet the high standards required for a successful product in the consumer market.

With that said, his reviews are not only widely read but also widely referred to on other websites, which in turn created an enormous and direct traffic flow to our campaign page. I understand that over thirty separate sites used data, information, or images from his review, which would have generated significant traffic directly back to our campaign page.

Unfortunately, Kickstarter statistics do not measure this flow on traffic. However, we feel there would have been at least a 5x multiple of sales due to the review by DCR.

Again, I stress that if DCR hadn't liked our product, he would have said it loud and clear to his (and our) audience. I'm pretty confident that we would have had 0 percent sales via DCR on our Kickstarter statistics!

What does all this mean in relation to marketing and influencers? We approached DCR to join us in the development of the product by sending him the earliest proto-types and subsequent versions of our products during the development phase. We asked if he would look at them, try them out, provide feedback, and keep everything embargoed until we were ready. In this case, it was being ready for the launch of the Kickstarter campaign. In the case of Fly6, we managed to get an almost final version of the product to him just before our Kickstarter campaign launched. See the review here: **https://www.dcrainmaker.com/2014/02/fly6-hd-camera-light.Html**.

As it happened, he liked the concept, execution, and product—but most of all, he liked that he got a real sample/prototype to use and evaluate for himself. This was something (which he stressed in his review) that was critical for him before he would even consider doing a review on his popular site. Ray has told me personally that he would never do a proper review on a product just based on a media release or Kickstarter campaign other than to voice his opinion on what he sees.

DC RAINMAKER

First Look At Fly6 HD Camera & Tail-Light Combo

How important was his review? In the Kickstarter back end statistics, it tells you how many backers came from various sites. In the case of Fly6, 3 per-cent (around $8,000 worth of pledges) of all the backers came directly from the DCR website. This is pretty significant and shows the direct monetary value of his review.

PRO TIP

Select the top few influencers in your space and appeal to them to be part of your product development journey

Post the Kickstarter campaign, we kept sending DCR prototypes and new versions as we developed more products. His critical feedback on the products and their features and functions was fantastic. He had a solid finger on the pulse of the sports tech industry, where it was going, and what his readers liked, which he mashed all together to help us with product refinements during development.

DCR has a massive group of dedicated readers of his blog, and these people are almost a perfect match for our intended customers. This is why we engaged DCR early, provided real prototypes, and let him do his thing—warts and all! He does not keep the prototypes, nor does he accept any funds/payments from manufacturers.

We also selected other influencers who we thought would address our intended customer base and provided working samples. The reviews that all of these people provided were much more authentic than a reworded—or worse, a regurgitated—media release using a standard photo set. In their world, original and genuine content is critical for them (and whoever they report to), so make their jobs easier and make sure you give them something real to write about, or else they are likely to not write about it at all. When a journo from Wired magazine writes about your product—having used it before any media announcement—that's powerful, and that's what I would recommend you strive for.

PRO TIP Make sure you provide something physical to these influencers. For hardware projects, it's self-evident on what you need to send them. With software projects, be creative, send them your software on a thumb drive with a poster or handwritten letter.

Practically speaking, you can't select a bunch of people to join the product development journey with you, mainly because you just don't have enough prototypes to go around. Look at your best influencers in the space you are playing in, select the top two to three (if you can supply them with the prototypes), and immerse them in your product development journey (if they agree to come along for the ride, most will enjoy the process).

With all the other journos, plan ahead to make extra prototypes. We aim to have between twenty and forty units, depending on the product and cost of prototypes. You can send out extras to the next tier of journos/bloggers, who you can ask to test it out (under embargo) before publishing their review of it on your deemed release date.

I should say, as well, that if you are asking these people for their feedback, don't take it lightly. If they are kind enough to give you genuine feedback (negative or positive), raise that feedback at the product development meetings and seriously consider implementing it. Not only will it give the person enormous satisfaction to see their suggestion manifest in the next prototype, it will show them that you mean business in creating a product that addresses the real needs of your customers. This should show up in the tone of their reviews and help put a positive light on the piece they write about your product.

In my opinion, this is how you market your product in the best possible way for your crowdfunding campaigns and beyond.

BONUS CONTENT: Sample Tracking

The bonus content from chapter 7 directly relates to the content in this chapter and should be used to manage and monitor what I feel is your most powerful marketing tool, product samples being used by top influencers.

VIDEO

THERE IS an interesting quote that goes like this:

> *❝ In life, there are four things you can't get back: the stone after the throw, the word after it's said, the action after it's done, and the time after it has passed.*"

I feel I need to add to the quote as follows:

❝ The video after you have launched your Kickstarter campaign!❞

It might not need to be said, but sometimes it's important to state the obvious—the video is one of the most important components of your campaign. However, what many people don't know is that you need to consider this fundamental component in many different ways.

Once your campaign goes live, you will have created a video that will be available on the internet forever. Did I mention, forever? If you are hoping to create a business from your project then you have to consider if—in the future when your business is thriving—this video might get dragged up from the archives and cause any brand damage. Videos don't go away, and Kickstarter videos are usually at the top of search queries, so expect it to be readily found.

In reality, your video should be one of your strongest marketing tools given it is at the start of every campaign. It's possibly going to be the most shared feature (along with your main campaign image) of your campaign. Therefore, it needs to be one of the strongest features, delivering the typical pitch (problem, solution, and call to action) in the most succinct fashion that addresses your audience's sensibilities. Let me break that down for you.

It does not take much deep thinking to realize that if you can deliver your full message or pitch in one minute, it is likely to get viewed more than if you delivered the same message but with more detail in, say, two minutes. People are time poor, and statistics will show that your video will get viewed by many people. However, the vast majority of them won't even finish watching it (no matter how long or short it is).

With this in mind, it is very important to get your pitch completed within the video as soon as possible. If you are planning to provide something funny, informative, or details about your rewards that takes a little more time, make sure it comes after your call to action.

There is much advice available in the internet about how long your crowd-funding video should be. However, I do recommend that you deliver the main call to action within ninety seconds and don't let your video go longer than three minutes. If you have to make your video long for some reason, two minutes and fifty-nine seconds is much, much better than three minutes and two seconds in the same way pricing of your products should be $249, not $250.

You are the creator of your project, and your offering is delivering something unique to your audience. Therefore, you should be in the best place to know exactly who your audience is. If you can clearly identify your audience to a specific demographic, you will be better placed to deliver your pitch to them. You can break them down by age, gender, geographical location, personal interest, association, or whatever measurement you deem appropriate. This will allow you to tailor your video to appeal to them so they are more engaged and more willing to follow your call to action.

CASE STUDY—FLY12 VIDEO

*For our first Kickstarter campaign for Fly6, we used a local (Perth, Western Australian) creative firm, Kiosk Creative (****www.kioskcreative. com.au****), who was the creative behind the funny and viral video, "Shit Perth People Say" (****https://youtu.be/ NpW1dv6rTgk****).*

Using a local firm was cost effective for our first foray into making a video but did not directly address our global audience.

We took those learnings from that, and in our next video used a US-based firm, Bedrock Marketing, headquartered in South Carolina (**http://bedrock.marketing/**), to not only write the script but to produce and film the video as well.

We had already established that our primary audience is male, between twenty-five and fifty-five years old, American, and has a bike that they ride on the road.

This is a pretty specific profile of our audience which helped us come up with the video script. As a result, we filmed our second Kickstarter video in the United States (remember that we are based in Perth, Western Australia!) to provide a familiar setting (as in cycling on the right-hand side of the road. In Australia, we use the left-hand side of the road) as you can see from the screenshot below.

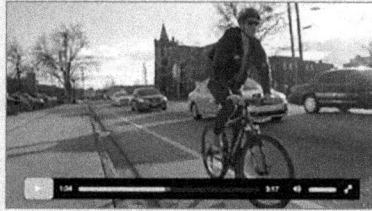

We also filmed some of the Fly12 Kickstarter video inside the garage of a typical American household where most of our target audience would have their bikes stored. Again, this provides the viewer a familiar setting which would encourage them to empathize with our offering and hopefully continue watching our video at least to see our call to action.

Bedrock Marketing also shot this video for us as well:
https://youtu.be/4_vqGKK20bE

CASE STUDY—VIDEO: DUO MOUNT

For our third Kickstarter campaign, we used a local filmmaker given the setting for the video was in a bike shop. A bike shop is relatively generic to geographic location, so even though our target audience was in the United States, the Perth-based location did not matter.

We did, however, use an American voice-over to better address our audience (https://youtu.be/2ateF8CtzyA) and give a small plug for the local bike shop (Wembley Cycles) that allowed us to take over their shop while filming the video.

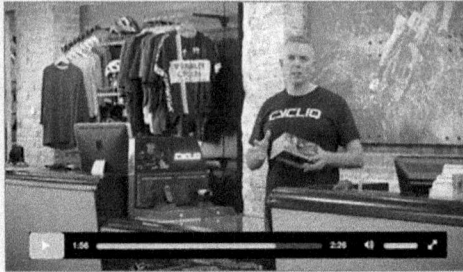

Backing a Kickstarter campaign can be compared to taking a bet on a horse race. There is risk. However, if you went to the races and placed a bet, and then went to look at the horse you bet on, if the horse looked skittish, lame, or nervous, you would probably rethink your decision to place the bet. Similarly, you are not likely to pledge your money on a project where you didn't get to see the creator to assess him or her for yourself. Does the creator give you the confidence that he or she can deliver you a product? Are they giving you confidence to place that bet?

If you think like this while planning your video, you will put yourself in the shoes of the person watching your video to provide a more compelling call to action. The principle I am talking about is this: you have to present yourself, the creator, as not only capable but motivated and dedicated to delivering the backer the product.

The minimum requirement to launch a product Kickstarter is a working prototype, which can be a significant achievement in itself. However, delivering finished versions of that product to hundreds or thousands of backers is quite something else. Simply adding money to a founder with a prototype does not equal successful delivery of what you pledged for. You, as the creator, have to demonstrate to the viewers of your video that with your ask hurdle achieved, you can and will deliver them their reward.

People that are browsing on Kickstarter are, generally speaking, actively looking to spend some money on a project. It is your job to help them select your project above others, so anything you can do in your video to impart your commitment to delivering them your product will go a long way to hitting your target.

Now I don't want to go in depth into the manufacturing process (I recommend reviewing chapter 5, "Manufacturing," or checking out the resources at **www.kickstartersuccess.com**. However, I am trying to show you that just within the prototyping process, there is a mountain of work to get through, and you need to demonstrate to your audience in the video that once you've achieved your ask hurdle, you will apply your knowledge, capability, and capacity to work through all parts of the process (prototyping, international approvals, packaging, shipping and logistics, team building, customer service, etc.) to deliver your fantastic product to their doorstep.

Credibility—or believability in you as a creator to deliver the product to the backer—is an essential outcome for your video and campaign.

CASE STUDY— PROVE YOU CAN DELIVER

With our first Kickstarter campaign (Fly6), we overcame this hurdle by working through all of the prototyping phases including two batches of 200 units of production prototypes. We used these units to send to product testers around the world.

This enabled us to test production processes, approvals, packaging, logistics, and shipping. Having many production prototypes also enabled us to send samples to many media and genre-specific outlets.

We found this made an enormous difference to our video message as we could not only prove with photos and videos that we had already made some units, we also could point the audience to the hands-on reviews from well-known persons and top-tier media in the cycling industry. These reviews validated our ability to not only make a good product but get it into the hands of our customers.

We demonstrated this fact clearly and purposefully in our video, which I feel was one of our strongest messages that resonated with our audience, leading to a very successful first campaign.

It's important to work with Kickstarter HQ on many technical details. However, a small detail like the video format, if you are hosting your video on the Kickstarter platform, needs to be compatible with their system.

PRO TIP If your video is going to be hosted by Kickstarter, make sure it's in a format that will work with them. Keep an open communication with them on these points as getting them wrong could delay your important launch day.

You might choose to host your video on Kickstarter's server or externally on something like YouTube or Vimeo. If you are hosting it externally, don't make the mistake I did. Leading up to the launch of our campaign, we only let a few select, external people have access to our video (as well as the versions of it leading up to the release version) by keeping the video settings on private. We used Vimeo at the time. We provided access to necessary people via a password to it so it wouldn't get leaked ahead of the launch.

The day of the campaign, everything was set for a specific launch time planned to the exact minute. And we pressed the Kickstarter launch button. We were very excited and were waiting for the money to come rolling in when we realized that the only thing I'd forgotten to do was to change the settings of the externally hosted server from private to public. The result was that, before I fixed it, the video did not go live for the first twenty seconds while I frantically tried to figure out why the video would not play on the campaign page.

PRO TIP Make a checklist of things to do on launch day. Include adjusting the privacy settings where your video is hosted so everyone can see your video when you go live with your campaign!

We found that the campaign video evolves all the time as you finalize design or add features to your product. Each time this happens, the video needs updating to have the latest information for your backers. Knowing this up front will enable you to better manage the process of finalizing the video for launch.

Knowing you have to get all the people to review the latest version of the video each time leading up to the launch date makes it easier to plan ahead. Expect to have the process of changing, reviewing, and amending the video to add some days to your program leading up to launch day.

There are some great resources on how to go about creating your video and what to include in it. I'd recommend starting off by checking out Kickstarter's own resource on this topic: **www.kickstarter.com/help/handbook/your_story**.

BONUS CONTENT: Prototypes Gantt Chart

The bonus content for chapter 11 addresses how access to prototypes will set the timing and revision for your Kickstarter video and campaign launch date.

CAMPAIGN PAGE

N o DOUBT you will have a website associated with your business or campaign. This is necessary for a number of things. But whatever branding you have within your website, do make sure that your campaign page carries the same branding.

Most people are going to do a little bit of research before pledging their money to your campaign. The first place they should find when doing this research is your website, so make sure you have your branding set and flowing across both platforms before you launch.

Cycliq Website

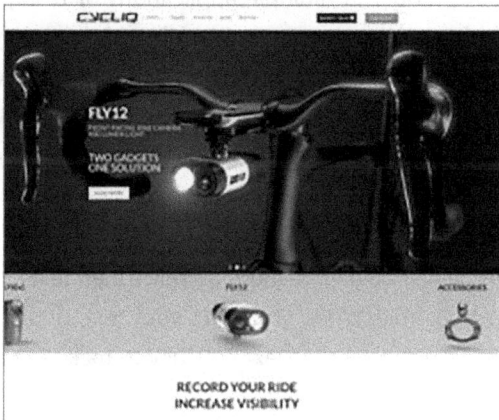

Fly12 Kickstarter campaign page

Keep your banding across your campaign page
and your webpage consistent

PRO TIP

Graphics, embedded videos, and GIFs (looping short videos) are increasingly used to promote campaigns. It makes sense because images and videos can relay more information in a shorter timeframe, and we know that our audience has a short attention span. This means you have to relay each message in the shortest time possible.

Photos of your product in multiple applications or being used as if they are completed products helps the backer identify with how they might use the product and should be used liberally throughout the campaign. Mostly use these within the campaign page, however add examples to your campaign updates or when answering backer questions in the comments section. The use of photos of your products is important for the backers to build belief that you can ultimately deliver them their reward.

Proportionally, you should have more graphics than text to make the campaign as simple as possible. When you write your text, understand who your target audience is, and choose your text carefully to make it easier for them to understand.

CASE STUDY—FLY12 CAMPAIGN BRANDING

In the case of our first campaign, where our target market were cyclists mainly based in the United States, we chose to use the American spelling convention. We used words like "finalized" as opposed to the Australian (and British) way of spelling it, "finalised".

*For our Fly12 and Duo Mount campaigns, we engaged our branding agency, The Black Eye Project (**theblackeyeproject.co.uk**) based in the United Kingdom, to make sure our campaign pages matched our branding objectives. We engaged them early on (around seven or eight months before we wanted to launch each campaign) and worked with them throughout the campaign as we made adjustments along the way.*

BONUS CONTENT: Kick-off List

Your campaign page should be a product of your branding and messaging, which should stem directly from why you are doing the campaign. The outcome of your campaign page will be specific to your brand and should be considered early on, which is why it is included in the content of the kickoff list.

BITS AND BOBS

THIS CHAPTER draws together many small topics I call "bits and bobs." They all form part of the important things you need to consider or implement to achieve the success you seek.

CURRENCY

For those of you doing a Kickstarter campaign from outside of the United States and with a US-based target market, you need to understand that not everyone outside of your country will be familiar with your currency, so when they are looking at how much your rewards are, they might not have an understanding of the value of your offering against their currency. The Kickstarter platform does not handle this very well even though they changed how currency was displayed from US dollars only to currency of origin (the country where the campaign was initiated), it still provides some ambiguity, particularly for United States citizens.

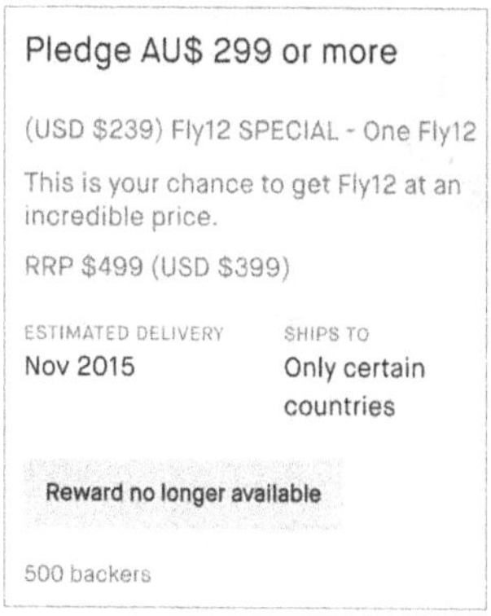

To overcome this, when listing your price simply add the equivalent amount in US dollars (see example, right) so that for people in the United States, they don't have to get out their currency converter or look up what it means to them.

Pledge AU$ 299 or more

(USD $239) Fly12 SPECIAL - One Fly12

This is your chance to get Fly12 at an incredible price.

RRP $499 (USD $399)

ESTIMATED DELIVERY
Nov 2015

SHIPS TO
Only certain countries

Reward no longer available

500 backers

The message here is to make it easy for your target market to understand how much they need to pledge for your product or offering. Always think of what you are saying as if you were your target audience.

SCAMS/WASTE OF TIME

Once you launch your campaign, you will get many "offers" pushed to your inbox to help market your campaign. Many of them will say that they have a database (no doubt full of "highly qualified Kickstarter backers") that they can send your campaign to if only you will pay them some amount of money.

We have tried a couple that we thought were genuine. However, the money would have been much better spent on Facebook advertising. My advice is to avoid these distractions and focus on marketing that you can manage while making sure you are reviewing results on an ongoing basis and refining your messaging along the way.

If you do succumb to paying for these lists or using some sort of EDM from a separate company, get them to back their claims. They will claim all sort of metrics and benefits. I suggest you use those claims to ensure a positive outcome.

I have provided a sample response (in chapter 8, "Lists and Databases") you can use for these offers you will receive. This fun and effective way of dealing with them should provide some light relief to you and the team during what should be an otherwise busy and intense time during your campaign.

PRO TIP Don't take on any of the marketing offers or buy into databases. Your money is better spent on Facebook advertising, which provided us with the best ROI.

TIMING

Setting the delivery date

When you are making a promise to deliver to your backers their reward, you are really making an agreement with each backer. While it may not be legally binding, it certainly is a very public agreement with each of the backers that should be morally binding. You don't want to break that agreement because it will be known forever that you did not deliver (review where I mentioned the Skully Kickstarter campaign in chapter 1, "Why").

Given this morally binding agreement you are making, I'd suggest when you set the delivery date in your campaign, spend some serious time to make sure you have covered off all of the manufacturing processes (see chapter 5) and have already got timing agreements with your factory.

Consider the following before setting your delivery date:

- Have you considered long lead time stock availability, and do those components require up-front payment? It affects your delivery date.

- If manufacturing in China, have you considered the impact of Chinese New Year (both in terms of component availability and production)? This can create up to eight weeks' delay in productivity as factory workers make the long trek back to their homelands so they can have three weeks with their family before making the trek back to the factory.

- Have you discussed capacity with your factory (what if they get another project before yours is to start, and then say they can't work on your project?)

- How sure are you that your project will get international approvals as they can sometimes take months to secure? Again, discuss these things early with your factory.

- Have you got your packaging designed so that you can add the approval marks at the last minute before production?

There are so many considerations to factor in that can affect your schedule. The above examples are just a few on the manufacturing side that could blow out your time line and are mostly outside of your control, which could lead to you breaking your promise to your backers.

Think carefully about what you are promising to your backers. Often you will want to get your backers their reward by some milestone date like Christmas—does that leave you any wiggle room in the event of a delay? These are all important things to think about before committing to delivery date.

PRO TIP

Add some amount of contingency to your delivery date. It is virtually impossible for everything to work on time. I would recommend adding around two months onto what you feel you will achieve for a delivery date. If you feel you can deliver in May, set your delivery date for July.

When to launch your campaign

There is loads of research addressing when you should launch your campaign. What time of day, what day of the week, which month—they all have some merit. However, each campaign is unique, and as such, you need to consider how your campaign can be optimized on a timing basis.

CASE STUDY—FLY12 LAUNCH TIMEZONE CHART

With our *Fly12* campaign, we knew our main market was based in the United States. However, we also knew our secondary markets as the United Kingdom and Australia. All three had significant time zone challenges. We wanted to launch our campaign at a time that would ensure that in those specific time zones—our backers —would be at least awake.

Our launch schedule against the main time zones looked like the figure below:

Timezones for Launch		
Location	Time	Date
Perth, AU	5AM	Feb, 13
Sydney, AU	8AM	Feb, 13
London, UK	9PM	Feb, 12
New York, US	4PM	Feb, 12
San Francisco, US	1PM	Feb, 12

While we feel we hit each of our target time zones, it did mean that the team had to come into the office very early (4a.m.) on launch day

If your target audience is US-based, don't have a campaign starting or finishing during Thanksgiving, Halloween, Christmas, Fourth of July, Black Friday, or Cyber Monday, as examples. Your potential backers are more likely to be busy doing something other than browsing on Kickstarter or thinking about pledging for your product. So, do a simple search for public or national holidays or major events in your target markets geography and work around any potential distractions.

How soon to start planning

In my opinion, you can never have enough planning for a Kickstarter campaign if your aim is to knock it out of the park. The aim, therefore, should be to start planning as soon as you can.

For our first campaign, we spent around three months planning, and for our second, we started around seven or eight months ahead of time. Depending on the nature of your product and what manufacturing process it requires, use this process give you a cue as to when to start planning your campaign. Do you have an engineering validation test prototype—this would be one that does what you want it to do but probably does not look very good? This could be the right time to begin planning your Kickstarter campaign.

PRO TIP You can't have a campaign without a working prototype. This should be the first point to consider when planning to set a campaign launch date. Your prototype will change a number of times leading up to your campaign so factor in that your video and campaign page might have to change with each change to the prototypes.

If you are planning on any less than a six-month preparation period for your first crowdfunding campaign, you are not giving yourself the best chance of success.

FRIENDS AND FAMILY

These are the guys that love you most. For sure, ask them to support you during the campaign but be sure that if you ask them, you need to fulfil the promises you are making. If you take their cash and don't deliver - you still need to see them at family gatherings or out and about…it's not good to take their money and not deliver. The same is true for the backers you don't know. Try and think about what you are doing from your own perspective, how would you expect to feel if someone took your money but did not deliver what they promised?

Use this as your moral compass when considering doing a crowdfunding campaign as well as the decisions you make along the way. This should help you have a successful campaign.

TO-DO LIST

When you first think you want to do a Kickstarter campaign, you need a to-do list as you start to work thought all the main components. The list should incorporate allocating tasks to each of your team members as soon as possible so they can start owning each important task.

CASE STUDY— PLAN AHEAD FOR UPDATES

When we planned our updates, we drafted four public updates to be released during the thirty-day campaign. We already knew when we were going to have factory visits, and so we planned updates around those visits. This is because we knew we would have some photos of videos to show in these updates.

In the updates, we tried to highlight production progress, images of the components, or tooling from the factory floor.

This list should be a living document in that after its initial creation, it should turn into an action list that gets updated every time you meet. Don't forget to allocate the task of updating this document and arranging the regular meetings to just one person.

One thing that often gets left off this list is the public and private campaign updates you should plan well before you launch your campaign. These planned updates could, and often do, change as you work your way through the campaign, but having them planned before the campaign starts is very important.

Your backers will want regular updates during the campaign, and given they have pledged their hard-earned money to your campaign, you should feel obligated to giving them regular updates or status changes as they occur.

That was just one example of a preplanned update. Other topics you can pre-plan for might include the following:

- Funding update ("yay—we made it" or "nearly there").

- Product improvements (you might be working on some product improvements but have not finalized them at the time you launch your campaign, but they might become available during the campaign).

- People—you can plan to do an update on the team behind the campaign and how hard they are working toward delivering the project on time.

- Urgency—only a few days to go creating a sense of urgency or fear of missing out.

CASE STUDY—DYNAMIC FLY12 CAMPAIGN

During our Fly12 campaign, we came up with the idea that Fly12 could act as a bike alarm (similar to a car alarm). We checked with our engineers that it was possible and asked them to test the concept. Luckily, it worked, and they gave us the nod.

Just like that we had an added feature to our offering that many of the backers loved. This was not known beforehand but created a great deal of buzz when we launched the update. We created an infographic (below) to showcase the feature and included it in a public and backer-only update. It was very well received.

Of course, things will change, and you might have more important updates to release during the campaign. However, having these preplanned updates takes one more component of the campaign from "what do we do here and who is going to do it" to "it is planned, prepared, and ready to go with small amendments." Trust me when I say that the more you prepare, the less stress you will have during the campaign.

PRO TIP Use a service like PR Underground (prunderground.com) to quickly and cost effectively push announcements ("we have launched" or "target in two hours" for example) out to the media. Make sure if you do this, you firstly inform the bloggers/media that are in your inner circle as they should hear each announcement before the public!

BE GENUINE

The growing Kickstarter community is built on trust. As a backer, you are trusting (and hoping) the creator is going to deliver the project and, thus, your reward to you. If you are not being truthful in any part of your campaign, you are not only risking your own credibility but also making it harder for those creators that will follow behind you.

Be honest, be open, and allow your backers to join you on the journey. Include the good, the bad, and the unexpected. Most backers understand the whole risk aspect of crowdfunding projects, so share your risks and be up front when you encounter things that will affect your ability to deliver on your promise. It could be timing or changes to the product itself. You will earn credibility in doing this, which you might need to draw on in the future, maybe not during the campaign but maybe later on when you have established your business when you might need to draw on that credibility for some other unforeseen issue.

KNOW YOUR AUDIENCE

It should be pretty obvious that you need to know who your audience is for your product. I'm suggesting that you need to know, intimately, who they are so that you can properly target them (this makes your marketing spend more efficient). Not only the demographic audience information but also the geographic audience are important to know as they affect how you manage many things from shipping and logistics through to financial considerations.

CASE STUDY–ADDRESS YOUR TARGET AUDIENCE

For our Kickstarter campaigns, we knew the three largest target markets were in the United States, United Kingdom, and Australia (in order of largest to smallest). Even though our product was generally for cyclists, we knew our audience well enough to know it did not appeal directly to European cyclists (where there are many more of them) because cycling in Europe is much safer. Therefore, cyclists are not as motivated to buy safety- related cycling devices.

We focused our efforts (visual appeal, language, currency, and launch time zones are just some examples) on the US market as it was the largest of the three target markets.

LEGAL

If you are not based in the United States, you will need to set up a bank account associated with you (if you are doing a campaign as an individual) or your company (if you are doing your campaign as a company). Kickstarter will verify that you have the account in the correct entity and do a small transaction in that account to verify it is active before your campaign gets approved.

This process can take up to two weeks so plan for this ahead of time—I would suggest you apply for this aspect with Kickstarter HQ at least two months before your planned launch date to avoid any problems. This way, if you have to create new accounts or need to arrange any legal documentation to get it finalized, you will have enough time to sort it out without affecting your planned launch date.

WEBSITE

Again, this might sound obvious, but you need to have a website well before you launch your Kickstarter campaign. This is where you can start building your database/list, explain more about who you are, maybe a teaser about the product you are going to launch. This should also be where you send people after the Kickstarter campaign to take preorders and continue to keep that cash rolling in.

PRE-SELLING AFTER

The different pathways you can go down once your campaign is completed are well documented. If you launched on Kickstarter, you can do a follow-up campaign on Indiegogo or other crowdfunding platforms to build on the momentum from your original campaign.

SELECTING YOUR PAYMENT PROVIDER

There are many payment providers you can use to sell your products online. My advice is to be careful and diligent on which one you pick. Be sure to ask them specific questions before you agree to sign up with them. The best way to illustrate this is by case study:

CASE STUDY—KNOW THY PAYMENT PROVIDER

With Cycliq, we did not use a secondary crowdfunding campaign for follow-on, mainly because we had an established website that we wanted to direct further customers to interact with. I do want to touch on a topic that I think is not well known but is very critical to receiving funds into your bank account if you choose to get further presales via your own website. This particular issue can really crunch your cash flow if not managed well.

If you are a first-time product creator and are wanting to presell your product, post-Kickstarter campaign, via your website, you need to carefully consider which payment gateway provider you are going to select. Note this is before you have the products to ship to your customers.

In this scenario, the larger payment gateway providers, like PayPal and Stripe, will not release the funds you raise through preselling on your website, until you have proved to them (based on their methodology of proof).

Imagine this: You set up your website ecommerce to receive funds, ask people to preorder, they place their order, the transaction occurs, but the money does not land in your bank account. Does not sound like fun, right?

When this happened to us, we were using PayPal, who only released 50 percent of the proceeds of the presale. When we queried them, they told us that because we had not shipped the unit to the customer, they were going to escrow (hold back) the other 50 percent of funds until we shipped the units to the customers. This was a major cash flow problem for us at the time, but PayPal were fixed in this position. I suspect that is why many Kickstarter campaign creators do follow-on campaigns with other crowdfunding platforms where the funds are released at the end of the campaign.

These payment transaction companies do this to cater for the fact that you have not yet delivered the products and there is a significant risk to the payment gateway providers that they might have to refund the person transacting on the presale item in the event that you don't end up delivering the goods or the goods are not exactly what they thought they were getting. If that prepaying customer has almost any sort of complaint, they will have their money refunded, and then the risk is on the payment gateway provider.

So, factor in the fact that if you need the funds from your presales post-Kickstarter campaign (and I'd hazard a guess that you desperately do need them), the payment gateway provider might only be releasing 50 percent of the funds to you until you actually deliver the goods to all your customers. Note here as well that the balance 50 percent of funds owed to you from the payment gateway provider can sometimes be delayed even after you have delivered the goods, sometimes by months (ours was just over two months) because they want significant proof that you have shipped/delivered the goods.

They will ask for a range of proof of delivery, such as photos of the finished goods (on pallets in the factory), shipping confirmation emails, tracking numbers for all shipments, and more. We found that we were always dealing with someone different at the payment gateway company and would, almost every time, have to explain all the evidence to each person each time making the process very frustrating.

As an early-stage startup, these funds are your lifeblood, and having a bureaucracy fumble around with them when they are rightfully yours can not only test your resolve, but you're your ability to finance the business.

This issue can be made worse if you have delays in manufacturing, which are almost always going to happen with first-time manufacturing runs. In this case, your final 50 percent of funds payment from the provider will be equally delayed. If you can get your payment provider to let you know the rules and timing before you begin, you will be better equipped to manage your business cash flow.

PRO TIP A solution some people are taking is to roll pre-sales onto other platforms like Indiegogo where the terms for receiving the funds from pre-selling are more aligned with the needs of a startup.

CONTINGENCY PLANNING

Launch dates can easily come and go if you are not prepared and have all the necessary approvals. You should have your ideal launch window set, based on the parameters mentioned before, but you also need to have a contingency set up in the event that there is a delay. Have some thought on an hour delay, a day delay, a week delay, and a month delay. These delays can be due to your product having some last-minute change that requires you to redo your video or campaign or photography or graphics, Kickstarter withhold approvals for some reason, website going down, key person getting sick or many other reasons. Try and consider these things and how you will deal with it before you go to your database with your set launch date.

Failure for Kickstarter campaigns sits around 65% of overall campaigns. There is a high likelihood of this happening so think carefully about what would happen if your campaign did not succeed. Having done three very successful campaigns, I can say that I had a high degree of confidence after our first success that if I applied our plan and thought through all the aspects of the campaign that it would not fail however, it did not prevent us from considering what if it did.

Some of the thinking needs to be around the big question I asked at the beginning of this book: why are you doing this? If it is to build the next unicorn business, then a failure on Kickstarter will always be out there. Any future investors will look at the campaign to assess market validation if you are seeking investment funding post campaign.

- If you failed because you set your expectations too high, then that says to the investor you are not realists.
- If you failed because you did not hit a reasonable goal, they will think your product is not a good market fit.

The failure is there forever, so plan, consider, and then execute all the steps, and you will be able to count yourself in the 35 percent of successful campaigns and give your business the best chance of success for the future. Plan for success, but understand that failure is a strong possibility.

COPY CATS

If you have a good idea that is relatively easy to manufacture, even if it is patented, you will find yourself being copied—particularly if you had a successful campaign. Believe it, think about it, and prepare for it. You often can't stop people or companies from copying your concept. Sometimes the copy can be exactly the same and sometimes just enough to get around your patent, but either way you need to be prepared for this.

I believe the best defense to this occurring is that you need to quickly establish your distribution network or selling channels so that when someone wants to buy your product (or a copy like yours), they find yours first. This is not easy to do but should become your mission as you enter the period after a successful Kickstarter campaign. If you think Kickstarter was busy or hard, step into fast-moving consumer good sales and see what it's like! With that said, if you can quickly establish your product into any major retailer, it will help prevent other brands coming into that retailer as the retailer would have already established that product category with your product.

If you are going down the direct (online) selling route, you need to establish your brand as having many reviews and a high rating using platforms such as Amazon. If you have the most reviews with positive ratings, your product will push to the top of the search listings if people are doing generic searches. This is one way to stay ahead of copycat products but will not stop them coming.

Each copycat product will likely be cheaper than yours, so you will need to show the benefits and higher quality of your product as the selling points. Building your brand is important to help buffer you against copycats.

The original Fly6 (on the left) and an almost exact replica of Fly6 marketed by Aldi UK (on the right).

Original Fly12 (on the left) and a copy product (on the right).

PRESS PACK

When Kickstarter campaigns are successful, or at least interesting, the press usually want to do a piece on it for their publication in the same way that bloggers want to write about it if your product or offering that is aligned with their followers.

Prepare for media to contact you or your PR agent (if you have one) to ask for more information. They might want to get a quote from the founder(s) or at least get a press pack.

A press pack can be as creative as you want. However, it should at least have the following:

- copy of the current media release (and previous media releases if you have any)

- copy of the Kickstarter FAQ but written using more marketing language than Kickstarter language

- access to your best marketing videos or images (make sure they are of the highest resolution or your professionally edited versions)

- a series of typical questions and answers about your product

- if your product is related to other products or needs other services for it to function, include links to where that information can be found.

PRO TIP Have all this stuff ready and available on a drive where you can instantly send an access link so the media have all the correct information and best possible images to do a write up with.

The above list is fully electronic, meaning you can send it to anyone, anywhere, instantly. When I said you can be creative, you might like to think of something physical you can send to media interested in doing a piece on your campaign. While this might sound like a slow way to get your message out, it can actually be of great benefit. Let me explain.

Sending something internationally via mail, depending on the method you use, can take anywhere from three to twenty days. If you send something to a blogger or media outlet that lands on their desk in say fifteen days, that is likely to be the time when they will be prompted to write something about your campaign. In most cases, Kickstarter campaigns have a flat period of funding during the middle part of the campaign (see chapter 2 "People and Workload," for our examples of the flat period), and any new media release during that time can significantly help boost awareness and subsequently backers pledging.

Perhaps sending secondary media snail mail just after you launch with a physical press pack could deliver a much needed mid-campaign media boost to your campaign if any of the media pick up on the story you present to them. The fact that it is physical will provide a point of difference over the many, many electronic submissions they receive every day.

PRO TIP Don't rule out sending something physical (poster, sticker, thumb drive or whatever) to important media via snail mail as it can create a much-needed boost during the slow part of your campaign.

LAUNCH DAY

In theory, launch day is the day where all the planning, preparation, and hard work from you and your team come together. If you have addressed all the components within this book, you should feel confident, prepared, but mostly excited. Given the momentous occasion of this day, if you already have a full-time job (separate to the Kickstarter campaign), you should probably take this day off not only to give you the time you need but also to savor the day and enjoy it as much as possible with those that have helped you get to this point.

As mentioned before, you can never prepare enough, and with the excitement of launch day upon you, it's prudent to create a to-do list for this special day to make sure you get all the important things done. A sample launch-day to-do list is available in the bonus content you can access from **www.kickstartersuccess. com**.

You should have sent the last EDM to your database either yesterday or a few hours ago (depending on what works for your campaign), informing them of the exact time of the launch. This is very important, especially if you have early bird reward tiers, as you want to provide the best opportunities to your list over and above random people discovering your campaign. To be clear, the people on the list have given you something (their email addresses), and this is your chance to give them something back, which builds your relationship with them.

CASE STUDY - IMPORTANCE OF FAST LAUNCH

In the case of both Fly12 and Duo Mount campaigns, we hit our Ask Hurdle ($245,000 and $20,000 respectively) within 2.5 hours which triggered a series of tasks we didn't expect to do. Mainly doing updates on Kickstarter and our other networks (inner circle, social channels, media list and databases) with messages like "we have hit our target".

While both campaigns hit their target in very short timeframes, Fly12 was significant because of the sheer volume and value of pledges in that short timeframe was somewhat of a record at the time. In fact, Kicktraq, had our campaign trending at over $20M at one point.

Given how well the campaign was doing, we reached out to our Kickstarter HQ contact who checked out the campaign and soon after, we were awarded a 'Staff Pick' badge which helped boost further pledges. This also led on to further updates across all our platforms, the need to update our graphics to add the badge to show off our achievement.

This shows the power of a fast start that can only happen when you, your team and consultants working on the campaign, plan, prepare and execute on the content of this book.

PRO TIP

Make sure you disable privacy settings on your video if hosted on an external platform before launching your crowdfunding campaign!

From just after you press the launch button through to the end of the campaign, your focus should be on addressing all the comments that should be flowing through on both Kickstarter comments section as well as social media and personal channels. If you have allocated this task to one person on your team, as we did, it will be important for one of the main owners of the campaign (founder or founders) to work closely with that person for the first few posts to get the tone and style locked down based on what sort of queries are coming through.

Launch day for our three campaigns was always filled with excitement and anticipation. Sometimes our thoughts ran away from us (particularly with Fly12, when Kicktraq predicted our campaign to raise over $20 million on current trend after two hours of the campaign launch), but for the most part, those days were a celebration of the effort and dedication of all those involved—moments I cherish and remember fondly.

BONUS CONTENT: Bits and Bobs

This chapter addresses many topics which relate to some of the bonus content throughout the book. This bonus content sheet is a list of the subtopics and a few templates to assist you to ensure you have covered off each of them in your planning and preparation. In addition, I have included our very own launch-day running sheet so you can see how we ran out last Kickstarter launch from an hour beforehand to an hour after we pressed the launch button.

THANK YOU

CONGRATULATIONS for reading my book and taking the first major step in your journey to launch your crowdfunding campaign. I hope you are now fully armed with the necessary tactics to not only hit your crowdfunding goals but also have a successful campaign in delivering your awesome products to your backers.

Within the book I refer to bonus content for you to print out and use as worksheets and templates to assist when you work through each chapter in detail with your campaign team, providing a bunch of resources and services I have either used myself or recommend you use to help you improve your chances of success. All this is available for free from **www.kickstartersuccess.com**.

Where is Cycliq today?

Cycliq are delivering leading edge technology that combine leading edge video camera and lighting in a compact piece of kit that have the longest run times in the action camera industry. These products act as a dash-cam for cyclists but also capture some of the best action videos you have ever seen from a bicycle. Check out their latest products: **cycliq.com**.

Fly6 CE

Full HD video camera and 100 lumen flashing red rear facing light for cyclists

Fly12 CE

Full HD video camera and 600 lumen flashing front facing light for cyclists

ABOUT THE AUTHOR

ANDREW **H**AGEN has been working on his own businesses since 2002, starting off in property development but also investing in leading edge sustainable technology. Originally a high school dropout, Andrew went back to school at age twenty-four to finish his high school studies before being accepted to university where he completed a Bachelor of Business with a double major in property and finance.

A colleague and eventual mentor recommended reading Robert Kiyosaki's book, *Rich Dad Poor Dad*, not long after having his first child, it inspired him to shoot for more than just working for someone else. He then formed a business with a good friend he met when finishing his high school studies. The business was based on property development (which was Andrew's full-time career at the time) and aimed at creating a supplementary income and ultimately a self-sustaining revenue stream.

Fast-forward ten years to 2012 and Andrew along with his friend and business partner are now keen cyclists, having picked up the sport since training to climb Mt. Kilimanjaro in 2007. One day, his friend was riding his bike by himself when some young guys drove up next to him, leaned out the passenger window, and shot him in the butt with an elastic slingshot from point-blank range, laughed at him, and then drove off, leaving his friend with a massive bruise on his butt and bewilderment as to what just happened. The car had driven off, so he could not get the license plate number, thus they got away with the assault.

This event led to the concept of having a rear-facing camera on the bike so that if something like that happened again, at least he would have the details of the car, including license plate, to pursue the offenders. Andrew and his friend discussed the concept and agreed that such a camera, along with an integrated light, would be a good product for cyclists. This was the genesis of Fly6, a rear-facing HD camera with integrated flashing red light for cyclists.

They both developed the product by pouring all their time and money into it up to the point where they had made four hundred preproduction units that they had sent all over the world for testing and feedback. The results were outstanding and the feedback very, very positive. In fact, one of the people testing the units had a major crash while using Fly6, and its footage enabled him to recover all the costs of his expensive medical bills as well as replacing his completely damaged bike—the ultimate endorsement that the product worked and helped vulnerable cyclists.

They knew they were onto a good thing, and having spent the best part of $450,000 to that point in time (late 2013), they really wanted to proceed with their first mass production run (three thousand units) but to do so would have cost substantially more at a time when they had used all of the available money they could find. The concept to run a Kickstarter campaign was raised but dismissed originally because it was a very public process. They didn't want anyone to copy the idea of our product at such an early stage of the business's development. In addition, Kickstarter was a relatively unknown system at that time.

Fast-forward a couple of months of consternation as to how to proceed with the business and a number of knock-backs from traditional forms of funding (banks) and they looked again to Kickstarter and agreed to launch a campaign.

Well, what happened from there is now well known—three Kickstarter campaigns, each at least 270 percent oversubscribed and raising in total over $1 million, which ultimately led to the business being listed on the Australian stock exchange.

Andrew is married and the father of five children living in his city of birth, Perth, Western Australia. He no longer works at Cycliq (but is still a significant shareholder) and now spends his time helping other startups grow their businesses globally, guiding businesses needing manufacturing in China, keynote public speaking at events, and spending time with his wife and children. For more information, check out **www.kickstartersuccess.com**.

www.ingramcontent.com/pod-product-compliance
Lightning Source LLC
Chambersburg PA
CBHW061335220326
41599CB00026B/5192